Henry

The Metrical History of Sir William Wallace, Knight of Ellerslie

Vol. III.

Henry

The Metrical History of Sir William Wallace, Knight of Ellerslie
Vol. III.

ISBN/EAN: 9783337020385

Printed in Europe, USA, Canada, Australia, Japan

Cover: Foto ©ninafisch / pixelio.de

More available books at **www.hansebooks.com**

THE
METRICAL HISTORY

OF

Sir WILLIAM WALLACE,

KNIGHT OF ELLERSLIE,

BY

HENRY,

COMMONLY CALLED

BLIND HARRY:

CAREFULLY TRANSCRIBED FROM THE M. S. COPY

OF THAT WORK, IN THE

ADVOCATES' LIBRARY,

UNDER THE EYE OF THE

EARL OF BUCHAN.

AND NOW PRINTED FOR THE FIRST TIME,

ACCORDING TO THE ANCIENT AND TRUE ORTHOGRAPHY.

WITH NOTES AND DISSERTATIONS.

IN THREE VOLUMES.

VOL. III.

"A! Fredome is a nobill thing!
"Fredome maks a man to have lykinge,
"Fredome all folace to men gives,
"He lives at efe that freely lives!

BARBOUR'S BRUS.

PERTH:

PRINTED BY R. MORISON JUNIOR,

FOR R. MORISON AND SON, BOOKSELLERS; PERTH.

M,DCC,XC.

THE

L I F E

OF

SIR WILLIAM WALLACE, &c.

BOOK X.

Battle of Falkirk, 1298—Loft by Diffenfion—Wallace and
Bruce Fight—Death of Graham—Wallace Kills 30,000
Englifh—Wallace and Bruce confer—Wallace attacks the
Englifh by Night—Frees Scotland a Second Time—Goes
again to France—Kills John of Lyne—Made Lord of
Guienne—King Edward Conquers Scotland.

YIS Wodftok raid into ye north gud fpeid,
　　Off Scotts as yan he had bot litill dreid ;
For weill he trowit for to refkew Dunde.
Yar fchippis com to Tay in be ye fe.
Hys gydys faid, yai fuld hym gydyn by　　　　　　5
Santt Jhonftoun, quhar was paffage playnly.
Ye hycht yai tuk, and lukyt yaim about,
So war yai war off Wallace and hys rout.
In fum part yan he ramordyt hys thocht,
Ye Kings cummaund becaufs he kepyt nocht ;　　10

VOL. III.　　　　　　　A　　　　　　　Bot

Bot quhen he faw yair war fewar yan he,
He wald yaim byd, and oyir do or de.
Schyr Jhon Ramfay formeft hys power faw,
He faid, zon is, yat ze fe hyddyr draw,
Oyir Sothroune, yat cummys fa cruellye,   15
Or Erle Malcom to fck yow for fupple.
Yan Wallace fmyld, and faid, Inglis yai ar,
Ze may yaim ken rycht weill, quhar euir yai far.
On Schyrrieff-mur Wallace ye feild has tane,
With aucht thoufand, yat worthi was in wane.   20
Ye Sothroune was rycht douchty in yair deid,
Togyddyr ftraik, weyll ftuffyt in fteyll weid.
Yan fpers all into fplendrys fprent.
Ye hardy Scotts throwchout ye Sothroune went;
In redy battaill fewyn thowfand down yai bar,   25
Dede on ye bent, yat recoueryt neuir mar.
With fell fechtand off wapynnys groundyn cleyn,
Blud fra byrneis was bufchyt on ye greyn.
Ye felloune ftour, yat awfull was and ftrang,
Ye worthi Scotts fo felloune on yaim dang,   30
At all was dede within a litill ftound,
Nayn off yat place had power for to found.
Zong Wodftok has bath land and lyff forlorn.
Ye Scotts fpulzied off gud ner yaim beforn,
Quhat yaim thocht beft, off fyn harnes yai waill, 35
Bath gold and gud, and horfs yat mycht yaim waill.
To Stirlyng Bryg, without reftyng, yai raid,
Or ma fuld com, Wallace yis ordinans maid,
Paft our ye Bryg, Wallace gert wrychts call,
He with crafts undid ye paffage all;   40

Sa

Sa ya fam folk he fend to ye Depe-furd,
Gert fet ye ground with fcharp fpykys off burd;
Bot nyne or ten he keft a gait befor,
Langs ye fchauld maid it both dep and fchor.
Yan Wallace faid, on a fyd we fall be,   45
Zon King and I, bot gyff he fouthwart fle.
He fend Lawder, quhilk had in hand ye Bafs,
Langs ye coft, quhar ony wefchel was,
And men with hym, yat wyfly couth luk,
Off ilka boyt a burd or twa out tuk.   50
Schyppys yai brynt off ftrangears yat was yar;
Cetoun and he to Wallace yus yai fayr,
In Stirryng lay apon hys purpos ftill,
For Inglifmen to fe quhat way yai will.
Ye Erle Malcom Stirlyng in kepyng had,   55
Till hym he com with men off armes fad,
Thre hundreth haill, yat fekyr war and trew,
Off Lennox folk, yair power to renew.
Schyr jhon ye Grayme, fra Dundaff priwaly,
Till Wallace com with a gud chewalry;   60
Tithands hym brocht, ye Sothroune com at hand,
In Forfychan King Edwarde was lugeand,
Stroyand ye place off purweans yat was yar,
Santt Jhonys gud for yaim yai wald nocht fpar.
Ye gud Stewart off But com to ye land,   65
With hym he ledys ma yan xii thoufand,
To cumyn paft was yan in Cummernald;
Apon ye morn bownyt ye Stewart bald,
Sone till aray with men off armes brycht,
Twentye thoufand yan femblyt to yair fycht.   70

A 2   Ye

Ye Lord Stewart and Cumyn furth yai ryd
To ye Fawkirk and yar hecht to abyd.
Ye Scotts Chyftane yan out off Stirlyng paft,
To ye Fawkyrk he fped hys oft full faft.
Wallace and hys yan till aray he zeid,   75
With ten thoufand off douchty men in deid.
Quha couth behald yair awfull Lordly wult,
Sa weyll befeyn, fo forthwart ftern and ftult,
Sa gud Chyftanys, as with fa few yar beyn,
Without a King, was neuir in Scotland feyn. 80
Wallace hymfelff, and Erle Malcom yat Lord,
Schyr Jhon ye Grayme, and Ramfay at accord,
Cetoun, Lawdir, and Lundy, yat was wycht,
Adam **Wallace** to yat jornay hym dycht;
And mony gud, quhilk prewyt weyll in prefs, 85
Yair namys all I may nocht her reherfs.
Sothroune or yan out off Forfychan fur,
Yar paffage maid into Slamanau-mur;
Intill a playn fet tents and palzon,
South hald Fawkyrk, a litill aboune **ye** toun. 90
And Jop hymfelff jugyt yaim **be** hys fycht,
In hall nowmyr a hundyr thoufand rycht.
Off Wallace com ye Scotts fic confort tuk,
Quhen yai hym faw, all raddour yai forfuk;
For off Inwy was few yat at it wyft, 95
Trefonable folk yair mattirs wyrks throw lyft.
Poyfone fenfyne at ye Fawkirk is cald,
Throw trefone and corruptione off ald.
Lord Cumyn had inwy at gud Wallace,
For Erle Patrik yat hapnyt apon cace, 100

        Cuntefs

Cuntefs off Nerch was Cumyns fyftyr der;
Undyr colour he wrocht in yis maner,
Into ye oft had ordand Wallace ded,
And maid Stewart with hym to fall in pled;
He faid, yat Lord, at Wallace had no rycht   105
Power to leid, and he prefent in fycht;
He bad hym tak ye wantgard for to gy,
Sa wyft he weill yat yai fuld ftryff for yi,
Lord Stewart aft at Wallace hys cunfaill,
Said, fchyr, ze knaw quhat may us maift awaill; 110
Zon fclloune King is awfull for to byd.
Rycht unabafyt Wallace anfuerd yat tyd,
And I haiff feyn ma twyfs into Scotland,
With zon ilk King, quhen Scottfmen tuk on hand.
With fewar men yan now ar hyddyr focht,   115
Yis realme agayn to full gud purpos brocht;
Schyr, we will fecht, for we haiff men inew,
As for a day, fa yat we all be trew.
Ye Stewart faid, he wald ye wantgard haiff.
Wallace anfuerd, and faid, fa God me faiff,   120
Yat fall ze nocht, as lang as I may ryng,
Nor no man ellis, quhill I fe my rycht King;
Gyff he will cum, and tak on hym ye croun,
At hys commaund I fall be reddy boun;
Throch Godds Grace I refkewyt Scotland twyfs, 125
I war to mad to leyff on fic wyfs,
To tyn for boft yat I haiff gouernyt lang.
Yus halff in wraith frewart hym can he gang.
Stewart yarwith all bolnyt into baill,
Wallace, he faid, be the I tell a taill.   130

A 3   Say

Say furth, quoth he, off ye faireſt ze can.

Unhappily hys taill yus he began.

Wallace, he ſaid, yow takis ye mekill cur,

So feryt it be wyrkyng off natur,

Quhow a Howlat complend off **hys** fethrane,　　135

Quhill **deym** natur tuk off ilk byrd but blame,

A ſayr fethyr, and to ye Howlat gaiff;

Yan be throuch **pryd** raboytat all ye laiff.

Quhar **off** ſuld yi ſenzie ſchaw ſe he,

Yow thinkis nane her at ſuld yi ſalow be;　　140

Yis marks it, yow ar cled with our **men,**

Had we our awn, yir war bot few to **ken.**

At yir wordis gud Wallace brynt as **fyr,**

Our haiſtely he anſuerd hym in ire,

Yow leid, he ſaid, **ye** ſuth full oft has beyn,　　145

Yar and I baid, quhar yow durſt nocht be ſeyn

Contrar enemys, na mar, for Scotlands **rycht,**

Yan dar ye Howlat quhen yat **ye day is** brycht;

Yat taill full meit yow has tauld off **yi ſell,**

To yi deſyr yow ſall me nocht compell;　　150

Cumyn it is has gyffyn yis cunſaill,

Will God ze ſall off your fyrſt purpoſs faill:

Yat fals traytour, yat I off dangyr brocht,

Is **wondyr** lyk till bryng yis realm till nocht;

For yi ogart oyir yow ſall de,　　155

Or in priſoun byd, or cowart lik to **fle.**

Reſkew off me yow ſall get nane yis day.

Yarwith **he** turnd, and fra yaim raid hys way.

Ten thouſand haill fra yaim with Wallace raid,

Nan was bettyr in all **yis** warld ſa braid,　　160

As

As off fic men, at leiffand was in lyff.

Allace, gret harm fell Scotland throw yat ftryff!

Paft till a wode fra ye Fawkyrk be eft,

He wald nocht byd for coummaund na requeft;

For charge off nane, bot it had beyn hys King,   165

At mycht yat tym bring hym fra hys etling.

Ye oyir Scotts, yat faw yis difcenfioun,

For difconford to leyff ye feild was boun;

Bot at yai men was natyff till Stewart,

Princypaill off But, tuk hardyment in hart.   170

Lord Stewart was at Cumyn grewyt yar,

Hecht, gyff he lyffyt, he fuld repent full fayr

Ye gret trefpace, yat, throw, raklefnace,

Had gert hym mak to Wallace in yat place:

For yair debait it was a gret pete,   175

For Inglifmen, yan mycht na trete be,

Haiftyt fa faft a battaill to ye feild,

Threty thoufand yat wei'l coud wappynys weild;

Erle off Harfurd was chofyn yair Chyftane.

Ye gud Stewart yan till aray is gane;   180

Ye feild he tuk, as trew and worthi Knycht.

Ye Inglifmen com on with full gret mycht.

Yair fell metyng was awfull for to fe,

At yat countour yai gert feill Sothroune de.

Quhen fpers was fpilt, hynt owt with fuerds fon, 185

On ayir fyd fell douchty deid was don;

Feill on ye ground was fellyt in yat place:

Stewart and hys can on hys enemys race;

Blud byrftyt out throuch maile and byrneis brycht.

Twentye thoufand, with dredfull wapynnys dycht,

Off

Off Sothroune men, derfly to dede yai dyng.
Ye ramanand agayn fled to yair King.
Ten thoufand yar, yat fra ye dede efchewyt,
With yair Chyftane into ye oft relewyt.
Agayn to ray ye hardy Stewart zeid,   195
Quhen Wallace faw yis nobill worthi deid,
Held up hys handys, with humyll prayer preft,
To God, he faid, gyff zon Lord Grace to left,
And power haiff hys worfchip till attend,
To wyn yir folk, and tak ye haill commend ;   200
Gret harm it war yat he fuld be ourfet ;
With new power yai will on hym rebet.
Be yat ye Bruce an awfull battaill baid,
And Byfchop Beik, quhill oft had been affayed,
Fowrty thoufand, apon ye Scotts to fayr,   205
With fell affer ; yai raiffit up rycht yair
Ye Bruce Banner, in Gold off Gowlis cler.
Quhen Wallace faw battaills approchit ner,
Ye rycht Lyon agayn hys awn kynrik,
Allace, he faid, ye warld is contrar lik !   210
Yis land fuld be zon tyrans heretage,
Yat cummys yus to ftroy hys awn barnage ;
Sa I war fre off it yat I faid ayr,
I wald forfwer Scotland for euir mar ;
Contrar ye Bruce I fuld refkew yaim now,   215
Or de yarfor, to God I mak a wow.
Ye gret debait in Wallace wyt can waid,
Betwix kyndnes, and willfull wow he maid.
Kyndnes hym bad refkew yaim fra yair fa.
Yan Wyll faid, nay, quhy, fuyll, wald zow do fa ?
                                        Zow

Zow has na wyt with rycht yi felfi to leid,
Suld yow help yaim yat wald put ze to deid?
Kyndnes faid, zha, yai ar gud Scottfmen.
Yan Wyll faid, nay ; werye zow may ken,
Had yai bene gud, all anys we had beyn,   225
Be refon heyr ye contrar now is feyn ;
For yai me hayt ma na Sothroune leid.
Kyndnes faid, nay, yat fchaw yai nocht in deid ;
Yocht ane off yaim be fals intill hys faw,
For caufs off hym yow fuld nocht lofs yaim aw ; 230
Yai haiff done weill into zon felloune ftour,
Refkew yaim now, and tak a hie honour.
Wyll faid, yai walk haiff reft fra me my lyff,
I baid for yaim in mony ftalwart ftryff.
Kyndnes faid, help, yair power is at nocht,   235
Syne wreik on hym yat all ye malice wrocht.
Wyll faid, yis day fall nocht helpyt be,
Yat I haiff faid, fall ay be faid for me.
Yai ar bot dede, God grant yaim off hys Blyfs,
Inwy lang fyne has done gret harme bot yis.   240
Wallace yarwith turnyt for ire in teyn,
Braith ters for baill byrft out fra bathe hys eyn ;
Schyr Jhon ye Grayme, and mony worthi wycht,
Wepyt in wo for forow off yat fycht.
Quhen Bruce hys battaill apon ye Scotts ftraik,   245
Yair cruell com maid cowards for to quaik ;
Lord Cumyn fled to Cummyrnauld away,
About ye Scotts ye Sothroune lappyt yay.
Ye men off But befor yair Lord yai ftud,
Defendand hym, quhen fell ftremys off blud   250

All

All yaim about in flothis quhar yai zeid.
Bathid in blud was Bruce fuerd and hys weid,
Throuch fell flauchtyr off trew men off hys awn,
Sone to dede ye Scotts was ourthrawn;
Syn flew ye Lord, for he wald nocht be tayn.   255
Quhen Wallace faw quhen yir gud men was gayn,
Lords, he faid, quhat now is your cunfaill?
Twa choyfs yar is, ye beft I rede us waill,
Yondyr ye King yis oft abandonand,
Heyr Bruce and Beik in zon battaill to ftand.   260
Zon King in wer has wyfs and felloune beyn,
Yair Captaynes als full cruell ar and keyn,
Bettyr off hand is not leiffand I wyfs,
In tyrandry, ze trow me weill off yis,
Yan Bruce and Beik to quhat part yai befet,   265
We haiff a choifs, quhilk is full hard but let.
And we turn eft for ftrenth in Lowthiane land,
Yai ftuff a chafs rycht fcharp I dar warrand,
Tak we ye mur, zon King is us befor,
Yar is bot yis withoutyn wordis mor.   270
To ye Torwode, for our fuccour is yar,
Throuch Bruce oft forfuth fyrft mon we far;
Amang us now yar nedis no debait,
Yon men ar dede, we will nocht ftryff for ftait.
Yai confent haill to wyrk rycht as he will,   275
Quhat hym thocht beft yai grantyt ro fulfill.
Gud Wallace yan yat floutiy couth yaim fter,
Befor yaim raid intill hys armour cler,
Rewll t fpers all in a nowmyr round
And we haive Grace for to pafs throuch yaim found,

And few be loft, till our ftrenth we will ryd,
Want we mony, in faith we fall all byd.
Ye hardnyt horfs faft on ye gret oft raift,
Ze rerd at rayfs quhen fperys in fondyr glaid,
Dufchyt in glofs dewyt with fpers dynt.　　285
Fra forgyt fteill ye fyr flew out but ftynt;
Ye felloune thrang quhen horfs and men remowyt,
Up draiff ye duft quhar yai yair richts prowyt.
Ye toyir oft mycht nocht no deds fe
For ftour at raifs quhill yai diffcuyryt be.　　290
Ye worthi Scotts aucht thoufand doun yai ber,
Few was at erd yat gud Wallace brocht yar;
Ye King cryit horfs apon yaim for to ryd,
Bot yis wyfs Lord gaiff hym cunfaill to byd.
Ye Erle off Zork faid, fchyr, yow wyrk amyfs,　　295
To brek aray, zon men quyt throuch yaim is;
Yai ken ye land, and will to ftrenthis draw,
Tak we ye playn we ar in perell aw.
Ye King confawit yat hys cunfaill was rycht,
Rewlyt hys oft, and baid ftill in yair fycht;　　300
Or Bruce and Beik mycht retorn yair battaill,
Ye Scotts war throch and had a gret awaill.
Wallace commaund ye oft fuld pafs yair way
To ye Torwode in all ye haift yai may;
Hymfelff and Grayme, and Laudir, turnyt in　　305
Betwex battaillys, prys prowy for to wyn;
And with yaim baid in vat place hundrys thre
Off weftland men was oyfet in jeperte,
Apon wycht horfs yat wefely coud ryd.
A flop yai maid quhar yai fet on a fyd,　　310

Na

Na spers yai had, bot suerdys off gud steill,
Yar within stour yai leit yair enemyss feill.
How yai full oft had prowyt beyn in press,
Off Inglismen yai maid seill to decess.
Or Bruce yaroff mycht weill persawing haiff,   315
Thre hundreth yar was traithyt to yair graiff.
Ye hardy Bruce ane oft abandownyt,
Twentye thousand he rewllyt be force and wytt,
Apon ye Scotts hys men for to reskew,
Serwyt yai war with gud spers enew.   320
And By schop Beik a stuff till hym to be,
Quhen gud Wallace yair ordinans couth se.
Allace! he said, zon man has mekill mycht,
And our gud will till undo hys awn rycht.
He bad hys men towart hys oft to ryd,   325
Yaim for to saiff he wald behynd yaim byd.
Mekill he trowis in God, and hys awn weid,
Till saiff hys men he did full douchty deid.
Apon hymselff mekill trawaill he tais
Ye gret battaill compleit apon hym gais   330
In ye forbreyst he retornyt full oft
Quham euir he hyt yair sawchyng was unsoft
Yat day in warld knawyn was nocht hys maik
A Sothroune man he flew ay at a straik
Bot hys awn strenth mycht nocht agayn yai be   335
Towart hys oft behuffyt for to fle
Ye Bruce hym hurt at ye returnyng yair
Undyr ye hals a deip wound and a fair.
Blude byrstyt out braithly at spers length
Fra ye gret oft he fled towart hys strenth   340
                                                    Sic

Sic a flear befor was neuir feyn,
Not at Gaddrys off ye Gawdy fer ye keyn,
Quhen Alexander refkewed ye Foryours,
Mycht till hym be comperd in yat hours,
Ye fell turnyng on folowars yat he maid,　　345
How bandounly befor ye oft he raid.
Nor quhow gud Grayme with cruell hardyment,
Na how Lawdir amang yair fayis went;
How yaim allayne into yat ftur yai ftud,
Quhill Wallace was in flanchyng off hys blud.　　350
Be yan he had ftemmyt full weill hys wound,
With thre hundreth into ye feild can found,　　:
To reikew Grayme and Lawdir yat was wycht;
Bot Byfchope Beik com with force and flycht,
Ye worthi Scots weryt fer on bak,　　355
Sewyn akyr breid, in turnyng off yair bak;
Zeit Wallace has yir twa delyueryt weill
Be hys awn ftrenth and hys awn fuerd off fteill.
Ye awfull Bruce amang yaim with gret mayn,
At ye refkew thre Scottfmen has he flayn:　　360
Quham he hyt rycht, ay at a ftraik was ded.
Wallace preyft in yarfor to fet rameid.
With a gud fper ye Bruce was ferwyt but baid,
With gret Inwy to Wallace faft he raid,
And he till hym, affonzeit nocht for yi,　　365
Ye Bruce hym myffyt as Wallace paflit by,
Awkwart he ftraik with hys fcharp groundyn glaive,
Sper and horfs crag intill fondyr he draive.
Bruce was at erd or Wallace turned about;
Ye gret battaill off thoufands ftern and ftout,　　370

Yai horffyt Bruce with men off gret walour,
Wallace allane was in yat ftalwart ftour.
Grayme preffyt in and ftraik ane Inglis Knycht,
Befor ye Bruce apon ye bafnett brycht,
Yat freualt ftuff, and all hys oyir weid,   375
Bathe bayn and brayn ye nobill fuerd throch zeid.
Ye Knycht was dede, gud Grayme retornyt tyte.
A futtell Knycht yarat had gret difpyt,
Folowyt at wait, and has perfawit weill
Graymes byrny was to narow fum deill,   380
Be neth ye waift, yat clofs it mycht not be,
On ye fyllat full fternly ftraik yat fle,
Perfyt ye bak, in ye bowalys hym bar,
With a fcharp fper, yat he mycht leiff no mar.
Grayme turnyt yarwith, and fmat yat Knycht in teyn,
Towart ye wefar, a litill beneth ye eyn.
Dede off yat dynt, to ground he dufchyt doun,
Schyr Jhon ye Grayme yat fwounyt on hys arfoune,
Or he ourcom till pafs till hys party,
Feill Sothroune men, yat was on fute hym by,   390
Stekyt hys horfs, yat he no furyir zeid,
Grayme zauld to God hys gud fpreit, and hys dreid.
Quhen Wallace faw yis Knycht to dede was wrocht,
Ye pytuoufs payn fo far thryllyt hys thocht,
All out off kynd it alteryt hys curage,   395
Hys wyt in wer was yan bot a wode rage.
Hys horfs hym bur in feild quhar fo hym lyft,
For off hymfelff as yan litill he wyft.
Lyk a wyld beft yat war fra refone rent,
As witlacewy into ye oft he went,   400

Dingand on hard, quhat Sothroune he rycht hyt,

Straucht apon horfs agayn mycht neu'r fyt.

Into yat rage full feill folk he dang doun,

All hym about was reddyt a gret rowm.

Quhen Bruce perfawyt with Wallace it ftud fa,   405

He chargyt men lang fperys for to ta,

And fla hys horfs, fa he fuld nocht efchaip.

Feill Sothroune yan to Wallace faft can fchaip,

Perfyt hys horfs with fperys on ayir fyd,

Woundys yai maid yat was bathe deip and wyd, 410

Off fchaftts part Wallace in fondyr fchayr,

But fell hedys in till hys horfs lett yair.

Sum wytt agayn to Wallace can radoun,

In hys awn mynd fo rewllyt hym refoun,

Sa for to de hym thocht it na waflage.   415

Yan for to fle he tuk na taryage,

Spuryt ye horfs, quhilk ran in a gud randoun

Till hys awn folk was bydand at Carroun.

Ye fey was in, at yai ftoppyt and ftud,

On loud he cryt and bad yaim tak ye flud;   420

Togyddyr byd, ze may nocht lofs a man.

At hys commaund ye wattir yai tuk yan.

Hym returned, ye entre for to kepe,

Quhill all hys oft was paffit our ye depe ;

Syn paffit our, and dred hys horfs fuld faill,   425

Hymfelff hewy cled into plait off maill.

Let he couth fwom, he trowit he mycht nocht weill;

Ye cler wattir culyt ye horfs fum deill.

Atour ye flud he bur hym to ye land,

Syne fell doun dede, and mycht na langar ftand. 430

R 2   Kerle

Kerle full fon a curfour to hym brocht,

Yan up he lap, amang ye oft he focht.

Grayme was away, and fyfteyn oyir wycht,

On Magdaleyn day yir folk to dede was dycht,

Threty thoufand off Inglifmen, for trew,   435

Ye worthi Scotts apon yat day yai flew;

Quhat be Stewart, and fyn be wycht Wallace,

For all hys pryce King Edwarde rewyt yat race.

To ye Torwode he bad ye oft fuld ryd,

Kerle and he paft apon Caroun fyd.   440

Behaldand our apon ye fouth party.

Bruce formaft com, and can on Wallace cry.

Quhat art yow yar? A man Wallace can fay.

Ye Bruce anfuerd, yat has yow prowyt to day.

Abyd, he faid, yow neds nocht now to fle.   445

Wallace anfuerd, I efchew nocht for ye,

Bot yat power has yi awn ner fordon,

Amends off yis will God we fall haiff fon.

Langage off ye, ye Bruce faid, I defyr.

Say furth, quoth he, yow may for litill hyr.   450

Ryd fra yat oft, gar yaim byd with Beik,

I wald fayn her quhat yow likis to fpek.

Ye oft baid ftyll, ye Bruce paffyt yaim fra,

He tuk with hym bot a Scott yat hecht Ra.

Quhen vat ye Bruce out off yair heryng wer,   455

He turnyt in, and yis queftion can fper.

Quhy wyrks zow yis, and mycht in gud pefs be?

Yan Wallace faid, bot in defaut off ye:

Throcht yi falfheid yine awn wyt has myfkend,

I cleym na rycht, bot wald yis land defend;   460

At

At zow undoys th ..h yi fals cruell deid,
Zow has tynt twa had beyn worth far mar meid,
On yis ilk day with a gud King to found,
Na fyffe mylzon off fyneft gold fo round,
Yat euir was wrocht in werk or ymage brycht,   465
I trow in warld was nocht a bettir Knycht,
Yan was ye gud Grayme off trewth and hardement.
Ters yarwith fra Wallace eyn doun went.
Bruce faid, fer ma on yis day we haiff lofyt.
Wallace anfuerd, allace, yai war ewill cofyt,   470
Throch yi treffon, yat fuld be our rycht King,
Yat willfully deftroyis yne awn offspring.
Ye Bruce afkyt, will zow do my dewyfs?
Wallace faid, nay, you leyfis in fic wyfs ;
Yow wald me mak at Edwardis will to be,   475
Zeit had I leuir to morn be hyngyt hye.
Zeit fall I fay as I wald cunfaill geyff,
Yan, as a Lord, yow mycht at lyking leyff,
At yin awn will in Scotland for to ryng,
And be in pefs and hald off Edwarde King.   480
Off yat fals King I think leuir wage to tak,
Bot contrar hym with my power to mak.
I cleym no thing as be litill off rycht ;
Yocht I mycht reiff, fen God has lent me mycht,
Fra ye yi croun off yis regioun to wer,   485
Bot I will nocht fic a charge on me ber.
Gret God waits beft quhat wer I tak on hand
For till kepe fre yat zow art gaynftandand.
It mycht beyn faid off ye lang tym beforn,
In curfyt tym yow was for Scotland born ;   490

B 3   Schamys

Schamys zow nocht, yat yow neuir zeit did gud,
Yow renygat, deuorar off yi blud;
I wow to God, ma I yi mayſtyr be
In ony feild, zow fall fer werthar de
Yan fall a Turk, for yi fals cruell wer,   495
Pagans till us dois nocht ſa mekill der.
Yan lewch ye Bruce at Wallace ernyſtfulnas,
And faid zow ſeis at yus ſtandis ye cafs.
Yis day zow art with our power ourſet,
Agayn zon King warrand yow may nocht get.   500
Yan Wallace faid, we ar be mekill thing
Starkar yis day in contrar off zon King,
Yan at Beggar, quhar he left many off hys,
And als ye feild; ſa fall he do with yis,
Or de yarfor, for all hys mekill mycht;   505
We haiff nocht lofyt in yis feild but a Knycht,
And Scotland now in ſic perill is ſtad,
To leyff it yus myfelff mycht be full mad.
Wallace, he faid, it prochys ner ye nycht,
Wald yow to morn, quhen yat ye day is lycht. 510
Or nyn off bell, meit me at yis chapell,
Be Dunypafs I wald haiff zour cunfell,
Wallace faid, nay, or yat ilk tym he went,
War all ye men hyn till ye orient
Intill a will with Edwarde, quha had fuorn,   515
We fall bargan be nyne hours to morn;
And for hys wrang reyff oyir he fall think fchaym,
Or de yarfor, or fle in Ingland haym.
Bot and zow will, fon be ye hour off thre,
At yat ilk tryſt, will God zow fall me fe.   520

Quhill

Quhill I may left, yis realm fall nocht for far.
Bruce promyft hym with twelff Scotts to be yar,
And Wallace faid, ftud zow rychtwyfs to me,
Countyr palyfs I fuld nocht be to ye.
I fall bryng ten, and, for yi nowmyr, ma,   525
I gyff no force yocht zow be freynd or fa.
Yus yai depertyt, ye Bruce paft hys way,
Till Lithgow raid, quhill yat King Edwarde lay,
Ye feild had left, and lugyt a fouth ye toun,
To fouper fet, as Bruce at ye palzoun   530
So entryt in, and faw wacand hys feit,
No wattir he tuk, bot maid hym to ye meit.
Faftand he was, and had beyn in gret dreid,
Bludyt was all hys wappynys and hys weid,
Sothroune Lordis, fcornyt hym in termys rud,   535
And faid, behald, zon Scott etts hys awn blud.
Ye King thocht ill yai maid fic derifioun,
He bad haiff watter to Bruce off Huntyngtoun.
Yai baid hym wefche, he faid, yat wald he nocht.
Yis blud is myn yat hurts maift my thocht.   540
Sadly ye Bruce yan in hys mynd remordyt
Ye words futh yat Wallace had hym recordyt;
Yan rewyt he far, fra refoun had hym knawin,
At blud and land fuid all lyk beyn hys awin;
With yaim he was lang or he couth get away,   545
Bot contrar Scotts he faucht nocht fra yat day.
Lat I ye Bruce fayr mowit in hys entent,
Gud Wallace fone agayn to ye oft went,
In ye Torwode quhilk had yair lugyng maid,
Tyrs yai bett yat was bathe brycht and braid;   550
                                                     Off

Off neit and fcheip yai tuk at fufficiens,

Yaroff full fone yai gat yaim fuftinens.

Wallace flepyt bot a fchort quhill and raifs,

To rewll ye oft on a gud mak he gais,

Till Erle Malcom, Ramfay and Lundy wycht,   555

With fyffe thoufand in a battaill yaim dycht.

Wallace, Lawdir, and Cryftell off Cetoun,

Fyffe thoufand led, and Wallace off Ricardtoun,

Full weill arayit into yair armour cleyn,

Paft to ye feild quhar yat ye chafs had beyn,   560

Amang ye ded men fekand ye worthiaft,

Ye corfs off Grayme, for quham he murnyt maft.

Quhen yai hym fand, and gud Wallace hym faw,

He lychtyt doun and hynt hym fra yaim aw

In armyfs, up behaldand hys paill face,   565

He kyffyt hym, and cryt full oft, allace!

My beft broyir in warld yat euir I had,

My afald freynd quhen I was hardeft ftad;

My hop, my heill, zow was in maift honour,

My faith, my help, my ftrenthiaft in ftour.   570

In ye was wyt, fredom and hardines,

In ye was trewth, manheid and nobilnes,

In ye was rewll, in ye was gouernans,

In ye was wertew withoutyn warians;

In ye Lawte, in ye was gret largnas,   575

In ye gentrice, in ye was ftedfaftnas.

Yow was gret caufs off wynnyng off Scotland,

Yocht I began, and tuk ye wer on hand

I wow to God, yat has ye warld in wauld.

Yi dede fall be to Sotheroune full der fauld.   580

Maryts

Martyr yow art for Scotlands rycht and me,
I fall yow wenge, or ellis yarfor to de.
Was na man yar fra wepyng mycht hym refreyn
For lofs off hym, quhen yai faw Wallace pleyn.
Yai caryit hym with worfchip and dolour,   585
In ye Fawkyrk graithyt hym in fepultour.
Wallace cummaundyt hys oft yarfor to byd,
Hys ten he tuk, for to meit Bruce yai ryd.
Sowth-weft he paft, quhar at ye tryft was fet,
Ye Bruce full fon and gud Wallace is met.   590
For lofs off Grayme, and als for propyr teyn,
He grewyt in ire, quhen he ye Bruce had feyn.
Yar falufyng was bot bouftous and thrawin,
Rewis zow, he faid, zow ar contrar yin awin.
Wallace, faid Bruce, rabut me now na mar,   595
Myn awin deds has bet me wondyr far.
Quhen Wallace hard with Bruce yat it ftud fua,
On kneis he fell, fer contenans can hym ma;
In armes fone ye Bruce has Wallace tane,
Out fra yair men in cunfaill ar yai gane.   600
I can nocht tell perfytly yair langage,
Bot ſis was it yair men had off knawlage:
Wallace hym prayit, cum fra zon Sothroune King:
Ye Bruce faid, nay, yar latt me a thing.
I am fo boundyn with witnes to be leill,   605
For all Ingland I wald nocht fals my feill;
Bot off a thing, I hecht to God and ye,
Yat contrar Scotts agayn I fall nocat be;
Intill a feild, with wappynys yat I ber,
In yi purpos I fall ye neuir der.   610

Gyff

Gyff God grants off us our hand till haiff,
I will bot fle my own felff for to faiff;
And Edwarde chaip, I pafs with hym agayn,
Bot I throw force be ayir tane or flayn.
Brek he on me quhen yat my terme is out,   615
I cum to ye, may I chaip fra yat dout.
Off yair cunfaill I can tell yow no mar.
Ye Bruce tuk leiff and can till Edwarde fayr,
Rycht fad in mynd for Scottfmen yat war loft
Wallace in haift prouidyt fon hys oft.   620
He maid Crawfurd ye Erle Malcom for to gyd
Ye Sauch-way till Enrawyn yai ryd,
For yar wachis fuld yaim nocht afpy.
Ye toyir oft hymfelff led haiftely
Be fouth Manwell, quhilk yat yai war betweyn,   625
Off ye outwatch yus chapyt yai unfeyn.
Ye Erle Malcom on Litl gow entris in,
Our haiftely a ftryff yai can begyn.
Wallace was nocht all to ye battaill boun,
Quhen yat yai hard ye fery raifs in ye toun.   630
On Edwards oft yai fet full fedandly,
Wallace and hys maid litill noyis or cry,
Bot occupyd with wappynys in yat ftour,
Feill fallen was dede yat was without armour.
All difarayit ye Inglis oft was yan;   635
Amang palzons ye Scotts, quhar mony men
Cuttyt cordys, gart mony tents fall,
Nan zon zeid yan, at anys fechtand war all,
Bot Wallace oft, and Erle Malcom with mycht.
King Edwarde yan, with awfull fer on hecht,   640
                                        Cryit

Cryit till aray, on Bruce, fo ſtern and ſtout,
Twentye thouſand in armys hym about
Into harnes had biddyn all yat nycht,
Bot frayt folk ſa dulfully was dycht,
On ilk ſid yai fled for ferdnes off oyir deid,   645
Wallace and hys fo rudly throw yaim zeid;
Towart ye King, and fellyt feill to ground,
Quha baid yaim yair rycht fell fechtyng has found.
Yat awfull King rycht manful.y abaid
Till all hys folk gret conford he maid.   650
Ye worthi Scotts agayn hym in yat ſtour,
Feill Sothroune flew into yair fyn armour,
So forthwarlye yai preſſyt in ye thrang,
Befor ye King maid ſloppys yaim amang.
Inglis commouns yan fled on ayir fyd,   655
Bot nobill men nane oyir durſt abyd.
Ye Bruce as yan to Scotts did no grewans,
A juge he was with fenzied contenans;
Sa did he neuir in na battaill ayr,
Nothyr zeit eftir, ſic ded as he ſchewd yar.   660
Ye Erle Malcom be yan into ye toun,
Ye Erle Herfurd to fle yan had maid boun.
Ye Lennox men fet yar lugyng in fyr,
Yan ferdly fled full mony Sothroune fyr.
Ye king Edwarde, yat zeit was fechtand ſtill,   665
Has feyn yaim fle, yat lykyt yaim full ill.
Ye worthi Scotts faſt towart hym yai prefs,
Hys brydell ner aſſayit or yai wald cefs.
Hys Banner-man Wallace flew in yat place,
And fone to ground ye Banner doun he race.   670

                                             Ye

Ye Erle off Zork cunfaillyt ye king to fle,
Yan he ratornd, fen na fuccour yai fe.
Ye Inglifmen haiff feyn yair Banner fall,
Without comfort, to fle yai purpoft all.
Elewyn thoufand in toun and feild was ded   675
Off Edwards folk, or hys felff left ye fted.
Twentye thoufand away togyddyr raid,
King and Chyftanis na langar tary maid.
Ye Scotts in haift yan to yair horfs yai zeid,
To ftuff ye chafs with worthi men in weid.   680
Ye Lennox folk, yat wantyt horfs and ger,
Tuk yaim at will, to help yaim in yat wer;
At Stragyll raid, quhat Scott mycht formeft pas,
Off Sothroune men quharoff gret fauchtyr was.
Wallace has feyn ye Scotts unordourly   685
Folow ye chafs, he maid Chyftanys in hy
Yaim for to rewll, and all togyddir ryd,
Commaundyt yaim ilk ane fuld oyir byd.
Into fleying ye Sothroune futtaill ar,
Se yai ye tym yai will fyt on us far,   690
Full fcalyt folk to yaim will fone ranew,
For ze fe weill yat yai ar men enew;
Ye folowars was rewllyt weill with fkill,
In gud aray yai raid all at hys will,
And flew doun faft quhat Sothroune yai ourtuk; 695
Contrar ye Scotts com neuir maiftrice to mak.
Into ye chafs hai haiftyt yaim fo ner,
Na Inglifmen out fra ye oft durft fter.
Ye frayit folk at tragill war fleand,
Drew to ye King weill ma yan ten thoufand.   700

Threty

Threty thoufand in nowmyr yan war yai,
Intill aray togyddyr paffyt away.
Feill Scotts horfs was drewyn in trawaill,
Forrown yat day fo vikyt can defaill.
Ye Sothroune was with horfs ferwyt full weill,   705
Off Wallace chafs ye Lords had gret feill ;
Off horfs yai war purwaide in gret wayn,
Ye King changyt on fyndry horfs off Spayn.
Yan Wallace faid, Lords ze may weill fe,
Zon folk ar now all yat zon King may be ;   710
For falt off ftuff we lois our mekill thing,
And we with horfs to pafs befor yis King,
We fuld mak end off all yis lang debait,
Zeit fum off yaim fall handelyt be full hayt.
Part off our horfs ar haldyn frefche and wycht,   715
Set on yaim far quhill we ar in yis mycht.
Yarwith ye Scotts fo hard amang yaim drew,
Off ye outward thre thoufand yar yai flew.
In Crawfurd-mur mony man was flayn,
Edwarde gart call ye Bruce mekill off mayn,   720
Yan faid he yus, gud Erle off Huntyngtoun,
Ze fe ye Scotts putts feill to confufioun,
Wald ze with men agayn on yaim raleiff,
And mer yaim anys I fail quhill I may leiff,
Lo ve zow fer mar yan ony oyir Knycht,   725
And for all yis fall put zow to zour rycht.
Yan faid ye Bruce, fchyr, lofs me off my band,
Yan I fal cum, I hecht zow be my hand.
Ye King full fone confideryt in hys mynd,
Quhen he hard Bruce anfuer hym in fic kynd,   730

Fra Inglifmen ye Bruces hart fet is,
Yan keft he yus, how he fuld mend yis myfs;
And fo he did, in Ingland at hys will
Na Scottfman he leit with Bruce byd ftill,
Bot quhar he paft held hym in fubjectioun   735
Off Inglifmen, held hym in gret bandoun.
He turnyt nocht, nor na mar langage maid,
In rayit battaill ye King to Sulway raid
With mekill payn faft apon Ingland coft,
Fyffte thoufand in yat trawaill he loft.   740
Quhen Wallace faw he chapyt was away,
Apon Annand agayn raturnyt yai
Till Edynburch, withoutyn tary mor,
Put in Crawfurd yat Captayne was befor;
Off heretage he had in Manweill land.   745
Wallace cummaund ilk man fuld hald in hand
Yair awin office, as yai befor had had.
Yus in gud pefs Scotland with rycht be ftad.
On ye tent day to Santt Jhonefton, he went
Semblyt Lords, fyne fchawit yaim hys entent.   750
Scrymgeour com, at yan had woun Dunde,
Wallace commaund yat tyme weill kepyt he.
He failzied fo, quhill ftrang hungyr yaim draiff,
Sa feblyft war, ye houfs till hym yai gaiff.
Ye wageourfs fone he put to confufioun,   755
Syne brocht Morton to mak a conclufioun,
Befor Wallace, and fone fra he kym faw,
He gart hyng hym, for all King Edwards aw.
Mafons, Minours, with Scrymzeour furth he fend,
Keft down Dunde, and yaroff maid ane end.   760
                                    Wallace,

Wallace, fadly quhen yir deds war don,
Ye Lords he caild, and hys will fchawit yaim fon.
Gud men, he faid, I was zour Gouernour,
My mynd was fet to do zow ay honour,
And for to bryng yis realm to rychtwyffnes; 765
For it I paffyt in mony paynfull place,
To wyn our awin myfelff I neuir fpaid,
At ye Fawkyrk yai ordand me reward.
Off yat reward ze her no mor throw me,
To fic gyfts God will full weill haiff E. 770
Now ze ar fre, throw ye makar off mycht,
He grant zow Grace weill to defend zour rycht.
Als I prefume, gyff harm be ordand me,
Yai ar Scottfmen at fuld ye werkars be.
I haiff enewch off our old enemyfs ftryff, 775
Me think our awn fuld nocht inwy my lyff.
My office our her playnly I refing,
I think no mor to tak on me fic thing.
In France I will, to wyn my leffyng yar,
A now awyfd, and her to cum na mar. 780
Lords gaynftud, bot all yat helpyt nocht,
For ony yar he did as hym beft thocht.
Byfchop Synclar was wefyd with feknas
Intill Dunkell, and fyn, throw Godds Grace
He recoueryt, quhen Wallace paft away, 785
Eftir ye Bruce he laftyt mony day.
Gud Wallace yus tuk leiff in Santt Jhoneftone,
Auchtand with hym till Dunde maid hym boun,
Longaweill paft, yat douchty was in deid,
Ye Barrounyfs fone off Brachyn with hym zeid; 790

Twa breyir als with yair uncle yaim dycht,
Symon Wallace, and Richard yat was wycht.
Schyr Thomas Gray, yis preift can with yaim fair,
Edwarde Litill, gud Jop and maiftyr Blayr.
Amang merchands gud Wallace tuk ye fe,   795
Pray we to God, yat he yair ledar be.
Yai faylyt furth by part off Ingland fchor,
Till Humbyr-mowth quhen at yai com befor,
Owt off ye fouth a gret rede faile yai fe,
Into ye top thre Leopards ftandand hye.   800
Ye merchands yan, yat fing quhen yai faw
Cammand fo ner, yai war difcumfyt aw;
For weill yai wyft, yat it was Jhon off **Lyn**,
Scotts to flay, he faid, it was na fyn.
Yir frayit folk zeid fone to confeffioun.   805
Yan Wallace faid, off fic deuotioun
Zet faw I neuir in no place quhar I paft,
For yis a fchip me think yow all agaft.
Zon wod-catts fall do us full der,
We faw yaim faill twyfs in a grettar wer.   810
On a fayr feild; fo fail yai on ye fe,
Dyfpyt it is to fe yaim ftand fo hye.
Ye fter man faid, fchyr, will ze undirftand,
Ile faiffs nane yat is born off Scotland.
We may nocht fle fra zon barge wait I weill,   815
Weyll ftuft yai ar with gun ganze off fteill.
Apon ye fe zon Rewar lang has beyn,
Till rychtwyfs men he dois full mekill teyn.
Mycht we be faiff, it forft nocht off our gud,
Yis wyfs he has, in fchort, for to conclud.   820

A

A flud he bers apon hys cot armour,
Ay drownand folk fo payntyt in figour;
Suppofs we murn ze fuld haiff no merwaill.
Yan Wallace faid, her is men off mar waill
To faill yi fchip, yarfor in holl zow ga,   825
And yi fers na mar cummyr as ma.
Wallace and hys yan fone till harnefs zeid.
Quhan yai war graithit into yair worthi weid,
Hymfelff and Blayr, and ye Knycht Longaweill,
Yir thre has tane to kepe ye myd fchip weill.   830
Befor us fewyn, and fex be oft us kend,
Syn twa he chefd ye top for to defend;
And Gray he maid yair fterman for to be.
Ye merchands yan faw yaim fa manfulle
To fend yaimfelff, becaufs yai had no weid,   835
Out off ye how yai tuk fkynnys gud fpeid,
Ay betwix twa ftufft won as yai mycht beft,
Agayn ye ftraik at yai fuld fum part left.
Yan Wallace lewch, and commendyt yaim aw,
Off fic harnes befor he neuir faw.   840
Be yan ye barge com on yaim wondyr faft,
Sewyn fcor in hyr, yat was no thing agaft.
Quhen Jhon off Lyn faw yaim in armour brycht,
He lewch, and faid, yir haltyn words on hycht,
Zon glakyt Scotts can us nocat undvrftand,   845
Fulys yai ar, is new cummyn off ye land.
He cryit, ftryk, bot no anfuer yai maid.
Blayr with a bow fchot faft withoutyn baid,
Or yai clyppyt, he fchot bot arowis thre,
And at ilk fchot he gert a rewar de.   850
              C 3   Ye

Ye bryggands yan yai bykkeryt wondyr faft,
Amang ye Scotts with fchot and gownnys caft;
And yai agayn with fpers hedyt weill,
Feill wounds maid throuch platts off fyne fteill,
Ayir oyir feftynyt with clippys keyn,   855
A cruell cowntyr yar was on fchip burd feyn.
Ye derff fchot draiff as thik as a haill fchour
Contende yarwith ye fpace ner off an hour.
Quhen fchott was gayn, ye Scots gret comfort had,
At hand ftrakys yai war fekyr and fad.   860
Ye merchands alf, with fic thing as yai mycht,
Prewyt full weill in defens off yair rycht.
Wallace and hys, at ner ftrakys quhen yai be,
With fcharp fuerdis yai gert fell brygands de;
Yai in ye top fo worthi wrocht with hand,   865
In ye fouth top yar mycht na rewar ftand.
All ye mid fchip off rewars was maid waift,
Yat to gyff our yai war in poynt almaift.
Yan Jhon off Lyn was rycht gretly agaft,
He faw hys folk fai'zie about hym faft,   870
With egyr will he waid haiff beyn away,
Bad wynd ye faill in all ye haift yai may;
Bot fra ye Scotts yai mycht nocht yan off fkey,
Ye clyp fa far on ayir burd yai wey.
Yai faw nathing yat mycht be to yaim efs,   875
Crawfurd on loft yair faili brynt in a blefs;
Or Jhon off Lyn fchup for to leyff yat fted,
Off hys beft men fexte was brocht to ded.
Yair fchip be ours a burd was mar off hycht,
Wallace lap in amang yai rewars wycht,   880

A

A man he ftraik our burd into ye fe,
On ye ourleft he flew fone oyir thre.
Longaweill entryt, and als ye mayftir Blayr,
Yai gaiff no gryth to frek at yai fand yar.
Wallace hymfelff with Jhon off Lyn was met,   885
At hys coler a felloune ftraik he fet,
Bathe helm and hed fra ye fchuldris he draiff,
Blayr our burd in ye fe keft ye laiff.
Off hys body, and all ye remaynand
Entryt, and flew ye brygands at yai fand.   890
Ye fchip yai tuk, gret gold and oyir ger
At yai reiffars had in gadryt lang in wer;
Bot mayfter Blayr fpak nathing off hymfell,
In deid off armes quhat awentur fell.
I Thomas Gray yan preift to Wallace,   895
Put in ye buk quhow yan hapnyt yis cace
At Blayr was in, mony worthi deid,
Off quhilk hymfelff had no plefance to reid.
Wallace rewllyt ye fchip with hys awn men,
And fallyt furth ye rycht courfs for to ken;   900
In ye floice hawyn quhill yat yai entryt be,
Ye merchands weill he kepyt in fawfte,
Off gold and ger he tuk part at yai fand,
Gaiff yaim ye fchip, fyne paffyt to ye land,
Throuch Flandrys raid apon a gudly wyfs,   905
Entryt to France, and focht up to Paryfs.
Ye glaid tithing at to ye King was brocht
Off Wallace com, it comford all yair thocht.
Yai trowit be hym to get redrefs off wrang
Ye Sothroune had in Gyan wrocht fo lang.   910

Ye Peryfs off France was full at yair parlement,
Ye King cummaund with haill and trew entent,
Yai fuld forfe a Lordfchip to Wallace.
Ye Lords all yan demyt off yis cace,
For Gyan was all haill owt off yair hand,   915
Yai thocht it beft for to gyff hym yat land;
For weyll yai trowit yai had fo wrocht befor,
He fuld it wyn, or ellis de yarfor;
Alfua off it yai mycht no profit haiff.
Yis was ye caufs to Wallace yai it gaiff.   920
Yis decret fone yai fchawit to ye King,
Difpleffyd he was yai maid hym fic a thing.
Off Gyan, yus, quhen Wallace had a feill,
No land, he faid, likyt hym halff fo weill.
My chance is yus for to be ay in wer,   925
And Inglifmen has done our realm moft der;
It was weill knawin my defens rychtwyfs yar,
Rycht haiff I her, my comfort is ye mar.
I thank your Lords maid fic reward to me,
Yair purpofs is I fall nocht ydill be.   930
Ye King bad hym be Duk off Gyan land.
To yat cummaund Wallace was gainftand,
Becaufs yat land was haly conquace,
Ile thocht to wyn erar throw Godds Grace,
Bot neuyr ye lefs ye King had maid hym Knycht,
And gaiff hym gold for to maynteine hys mycht,
Syn gaiff playn charge till hys wermen off France,
Yai fuld be haill at Wallace ordinance;
And als off hym he bad hym armes tak.
Wallace forfuk fic changyng for to mak;   940

Sen

Sen I began, I bar ye reid Lyoun,
And thinkis to be ay trewman to yat croun.
I thank yow, fchyr, off yis mychty reward,
Zour gyft herfor fall nocht rycht lang be fpard,
I think to quyt fum part ze kith on me   945
In your fcheruice, or ellis yarfor to de.
Gud Wallace thocht hys tym he wa'd nocht waift,
On to ye wer he graithyt hym in haift;
All Scottfmen yat was into yat land,
Till hym focht with yair fewte and band.   950
Langaweill als a gret power can raifs,
In Wallace help yis gud Knycht glaidly gais,
Ten thoufand haill off nobillmen yai war,
Ye braid Banner off Scotland difplayit yar;
Yir wermen fone apon Gyane yai fur,   955
Brak byggyngs doun quhilk had beyn ftark and ftur.
Sothroune yai flew agayn yaim maid debait,
Braithly on breid yai rafyt fyrs hait.
Schynnoun yai t uk at Wallace fyrft had woun,
And flew all men off Sothroune was yar foun.   960
Into yat town Wallace hys duellyng maid,
All yar about he wan ye contre braid.
Ye worthi Duk off Orliance was Lord,
Semblyt hys folk intill a gud accord,
Twelffe thoufand yan he had in armour brycht,   965
And thocht to help gud Wallace in hys rycht.
Leyff I yaim yus ye Duk and Wallace bathe,
And fpek fum part how Scotland tuk gret fcaithe.
Ye fals Inwy, ye wykkyt fell trefoun
Amang yaimfelff brocht feill to confufioun.   970

                                        Ye

Ye Knycht Wallang in Scotland maid repayr,
Ye fals Menteth, Schyr Jhon withoutyn mar,
Betwix yaim twa was maid a priwa band,
So on a day yai mett intill Annand.
Off ye Leyn-houfs Schyr Jhon had gret defyr.   975
Schyr Amer hecht he fuld it haiff in hyr
To hald in fe, and oyir landis mo,
Off King Edwarde, fo he wald pafs hym to.
Yus cordyt vai, and fyn to London went,
Edwarde was glaid for to hald yat payment.   980
Menteth was yar bound man to yat fals King,
To furthyr hym to Scotland in all thing ;
Syn paffyt haym, and Wallang with hym fur,
Quhill he was brocht agayn our Carleill mur
King Edward yan in ire and fers outrage,   985
Be threty davis raiffyt bys barnage,
In Scotland pafs, and yar na ftoppyng fand,
Na Chyftane yar yat durft agayn hym ftand.
For Menteth taid, yai thocht to mak Bruce King,
All trew Scotts wald be pleffyd off yat thing.   990
Zeit mony fled and durft nocht bid Edwarde,
Sum into Rofs, and in ye Ilis paft part.
Ye Byfchop Synclayr agayn fled into But,
With yat fals King he had no will to mut.
Yus without ftraik ye caftellis off Scotland,   995
King Edwarde haill has tane in hys awn hand,
Deuidyt fyne to men yat he wald lik,
Strenthis and toun to Rofs throuch yis kynryk.
Bathe hecht and waill obeyed all till hys will,
As he cummaund yai purpos to fullfill.   1000

                                    Ye

Ye Byfchopryks inclynyt till hys croun,

Bathe temperalite and all ye religioun.

Ye Roman, yat yan was in Scotland,

He gart be brocht, to fchaw quhar yai yaim fand,

And, but radem, yai brynt yaim yar ilk ane;   1005

Salyfbery oyfs our clerkis yan has tane.

Ye Lords he tuk yat wald nocht off hym hald,

In Ingland fend full nobill blud off ald.

Schyr Wilzam Lang Douglace to London he fend,

In ftrang prefoune quhar throuch he maid hys end.

Ye Erle Thomas yat Lord was off Murray,

And Lord Fryfaill fra hym he fend away,

Als Hew ye Hay, and oyir ayrs ma,

He gart Wallang with yaim in Ingland ga.

Na man was left all yis mayn land within,   1015

Fra Edwards pefs was knawin off ony kin.

Cetoun, Lawdir, duelt ftill into ye Bafs,

With yaim Lundy, and men yat worthi was;

Ye Erle Malcom and Cambell paft but let,

In But fuccour with Synclar for to get.   1020

Schyr Jhon Ramfay and Ruwan yan fled north,

To yair cufyng yat Lord was off Fyllorth.

Quhilk pafs with yaim throw Murray lands rycht;

Sa fand yai yar a gentill worthi Knycht

At Climace hecht, full cruell ay had beyn,   1025

And fayndyt weill amang hys enemyfs keyn.

He thocht neuir at Edwards faith to be,

Intyll hys tym he gert feill Sothroune de.

He led yir Lords in Rofs withoutyn mar,

At ye Stok-furd a ftark ftrenth byggyt yar;   1030

Kepyt

Kepyt yat land rycht worthely be wer,
Till yair enemyfs yai did full mekill der.
Adam Wallace, and Lindfay off Cragge,
Away yai fled be nycht apon ye fe,
And Robert Boyd quhilk was baith wyfs and wycht.
Arane yai tuk to fen'l yaim at yair mycht.
Ye Corfpatrik into Dunbar baid ftill,
Fewte full fone he had maid Edwarde till.
Abernethe, Lord Soullis, and Cumyn als,
And Jhon off Lorn yat lang had beyn full fals,   1040
Ye Lord Brechyn, and mony oyir baid
At Edwards faith, for gyftts he yaim maid.
Jufteis off Pefs for twentye dayis fet he
Off Inglifmen in Lorn, at men mycht be
Playn to declayr; bot, for yis caufs, I wyfs,   1045
Yat all Scotland be conquefs yan was hys.
Ye Lords yan, and Byfchop gud Synclar,
Sone out off But yai maid a Ballingar
To gud Wallace, tald hym yair turment haill,
Yan wrait yai yus to get help off yair baill.   1050
Our help, our heill, our hop, our Gouernour,
Our gudly gyd, our beft Chyftane in ftour,
Our Lord, our luff, our ftrenth our rychtwyfnas,
For Godds faik radeym anys to Grace,
And tak ye croun, till us it war kyndar,   1055
To bruk for ay, or fals Edwarde it war.
Ye wrytt he gat, bot zeit fuffer he wald,
For gret faliheid yat part hym dyd off ald.
Mekill dolour it did hym in hys mynd,
Off yar mysfayr, for trew he was and kynd.   1060

He

He thocht to tak amends off yat wrang,
He anſuerd nocht, both in hys wer furth rang.
Off King Edwarde zeit mar furth will I meill
Into quhat wyfs yat he couth Scotland deill.
In Santt Jhonſtoune ye Erle off Zork he maid   1065
Captayne to be off all yat landis braid,
Fra Tay to Dee, and undyr hym Butlar,
Hys Grantſchyr had at Kinclewyn endyt yar,
Hys Fadyr als, Wallace yaim bathe had ſlayn;
Edwarde yarfor maid hym a man off mayn.   1070
Ye Lord Bewmound into ye north he ſend.
Yai Lordſchippis all yai gaiff in commend,
To Sterlyng ſyn fra Santt Jhonſtoune he went,
Yar for to fullfill ye laiff off hys entent.
Ye Lord Clyffurd he gaiff yan Douglace Daill,   1075
Rewller to be off ye ſouth marchis haill.
All Galloway yan he gaiff Cumyn in hand,
Wyſt nayn bot God how lang yat ſtait fuld ſtand.
Ye gentill Lord gud Byfchop Lamyrtoun,
Off Santt Androwfs had Douglace off renoun.   1080
Befor yat tyme Jamyfs wycht and wyfs,
Till hym was cummyn fra fchulls off Paryfs.
A priwa fauour ye Byſchop till hym bar;
Bot Inglifmen was ſa gret maiſtris yar,
He durſt nocht weill in playn fchaw hym kyndnes, 1085
Quhill on a day he tuk ſum hardenes.
Douglace he cald, and couth to Stirlyng fayr,
Quhar King Edwarde was deland lands yar.
He proferd hym into ye Kings fcherwice
To bruk hys awn; fra he wyſt, in yis wyfs,   1090

VOL. III.   D   Douglace

Douglace he was, yan he forfuk planle,
Swor be Santt George, he brukis na land off me
Hys fadyr was in contrar off my croun,
Yarfor as now he bids in our prefoun.
To ye Byfchop nane oyir grant he maid,   1695
Bot as he plefd, delt furth yai lands braid.
To ye Lord Soullis ill haill ye merfs gaiff he,
And Captane als off Berweik for to be.
Oiyfant yan yat he in Stirlyng fand,
Quhen he hym had, he wald nocht kep hys band,
Ye quhilk he maid or he hym Styrlyng gaiff,
Defaitfully yus couth he hym diffayiff.
Intill Ingland fend hym till prifoun ftrang,
In gret diftrefs he lewyt yar full lang.
Quhen Edwarde King had delt all yis regioun,   1105
Hys leyff he tuk, in Ingland maid hym boun.
Owt off Styrlyng fouthward as yai couth ryd,
Cumyn hapnyt ner hand ye Bruce to byd.
Yus faid he, fchyr, and ze couth kepe cunfaill,
I can fchaw her quhilk may be zour awaill.   1110
Ye Bruce anfuerd, quhateuir ze fay to me,
As for my part fall weill confeillyt be.
Lord Cumyn faid, fchyr, knaw zow nocht yis thing,
Yat off yis realme ye fall be rychtwyfs King.
Yan faid ye Bruce, fuppofs I rychtwyfs be,   1115
I fe no tym to tak fic thing on me.
I am haldin into my enemyfs hand,
Undyr gret ayth, quhen I com in Scotland,
Nocht part fra hym for profyt nor requeft,
Na fer na ftrenth, bot gyff ded me areft.   1120

He

He hecht agayn to gyff yis land to me,
Now fynd I weill it is bot furcite;
For yus zow feis he dely myn heretage,
To othroune part, and iam to traytowris wage.
Yan Cumyn faid, will ze, to her, accord,   1125
Off my landys and ze lik to be Lord,
Ze fail yaim haiff, for zour rycht off ye croun;
Or and ze lik, fchyr, for my waryfoure,
I fall yow help with power at my mycht.
Ye Bruce anfuerd. I will nocht fall my rycht;   1130
Bot on yis wyfs, quhat Lordfchip yow will craiff
For yi fupple, I hecht yow fall it haiff.
Cum fra zon King, fchvr, with fum jeperte,
Now Edwarde has all Galloway geyffyn to me,
My neuo Soullis yat kepis Berweik toun,   1135
At zour cummaund hys power fall be boun.
My neu als a man off mekill mycht,
Ye Lord off Lorn has rowme into ye rycht.
My thrid neuo a Lord off gret renoun,
Will ryfs with us off Breichin ye Barroun.   1140
Yan faid ye Bruce, fayr yar fa fayr a chance,
Yat we mycht get agayn Wallace fra France,
Be wyt and force he couth yis Kynryk wyn,
Allace, we haiff our lang beyn haldyn in twyn!
To yat langage Cumyn maid na record   1145
Off ald deids intyll hys mynd remord.
Ye Bruce and he completyt furth yar bands,
Syn yat famyn nycht yai fellyt with yair hands.
Yis Ragment left ye Bruce with Cumyn yar,
With King Edwarde haym in Ingland can far.   1150

D 2   And

And yar ramaynyt quhill yis Ragment was knawin,
Thre zer and mar or Bruce perfewyt hys awin.
Sum men demys yat Cumyn yat Ragment fend,
Sum men yarfor agaynys makis efend.
Nayn may fay weill Edwarde was faklafing,   1155
Becaufs hys wyff was Edwards ner cufyng.
He ferwyt dede be rycht law off hys King,
So raklyfly myfkepyt fic a thing.
Had Bruce paft by but baid to antt Jhonftoun,
Be haill affent he had rafawit ye croun ;   1160
On Cumyn fyne he mycht haiff done ye law,
He couth nocht thoill fra tym yat he hym faw.
Yus Scotland left in hard perplexite,
Off Wallace mar in fum part fpek will we.

EXPLICIT DECIMUS PASSUS
ET INCIPIT UNDECIMUS PASSUS.

L I F E

O F

SIR WILLIAM WALLACE, &c.

B O O K XI.

Wallace Conquers Guienne—Ki 's two Champions—And a
Lion—Returns to Scotland—Fights at Elcho Park—Kills
Butler—And Five Men in a Foreft in Lorn—Adventure
at Rannoch Hall—Met by Several—Drives Beamont
from Aberdeen—Befieges Perth—Vallance engages Men-
teith to Betray Wallace—Edward Bruce in Scotland—
Wallace Betrayed at Glafgow—Vifion of a Monk concerning him—Beheaded at London.

YE fayr trawaill, ye ernyftfull befynes,
    Ye feill labour had in mony place,
To wyn ye land at ye gud King hym gaiff,
Intill hys ryng he wald no Sothroune faiff
In Gyan land Wallace was ftill at wer,   5
Off Scotlands lofs it did hys hart gret der;
Off trew Scotts in mynd he had pete,
He thocht to help quhen hys tym mycht fe.
Off fet battaillis fyffe he difcumfyt haill,
Bot jeperte, and mony ftrang affaill;   10

Syn

Syn yai forſuk, and durſt hym nocht abid,
Ye Sothroune fled fra hym on ayir ſid
To Burdeouſs in gret multiplye,
Yan com yai ſtufft with wittaill be ye ſe.
All Gyan land Wallace brocht till hys peſs,   15
To Burdeouſs zet he paſt or he wald ceſs.
On our byggyngs full gret maiſtyr yai maid,
Still ſaxte dayis at far failzie yai baid.
Fortrace and werk yat was without ye toun,
Yai brak and brynt and put to confuſioun.   20
Hage, alais, be lawbour yat was yar,
Fulzeit and ſpilt, yai wald na froit ſpar.
Ye Ingliſmen maid gret defens agayn
With ſchot and caſt, for yai war mekill off mayn ;
Off gownnys yai war and ganzies ſtuffyt weill,   25
All artailze and wappynys off fyn ſteill,
With men and meit within war buſkyt beyn ;
Yair gret Captayne was wyſs, cruell and keyn.
Off Gloſyſtyr yat huge Lord and her,
Yis Erle had beyn weill uſyt into wer,   30
Kepyt hys men with wytt and hardement,
Without ye toun yar durſt nane fra hym went.
Ye lands without wer ner waiſtyt away,
Wermen ſa lang into ye contre lay.
In Wallace oſt ſo ſcantyt ye wittaill,   35
Yai mycht not byd langar till aſſaill.
Yan yis wyſs Lord ye Duk off Orleance
To Wallace ſaid, ſchyr, ze ſuld knaw yis chance,
It ſtands our weill with yir fals Sothroune blud,
For on na wayis we can nocht ſtop yair fud.   40

Ye

Ye hawin yai haiff and fchippis at yair will,
Off Ingland cummys enewch off wittaill yaim till.
Yis land is purd off fud yat fuld us beild,
And we fe weyll als yai forfaik ye feild.
Yai will nocht fecht yocht we all her fuld byd,   45
Ze may off pefs plenyfs yir lands wyd.
My cunfaill is, in playn, anent yis thing,
At ze wald pafs with worfchipe to ye King.
Be hys affent ze may at lafar waill,
With prouifioun agayn for till affaill.   50
Wallace inclynd, and thankyt yis wyfs Lord,
Yan yai tranontyt all in a gud concord,
Paft up in France with honour to ye King,
And fchawit hym haill ye verite off yis thing;
And he yaroff in hart was wondyr glaid.   55
Franch men befor yat hundreth zer not haid
Off Gyan halff fa mekill into yair hand.
Wrytting be yan was new Cummyn off Scotland,
Fra part off Lordis and Byfchop gud Synclar,
Befocht ye King in yair termys fair,   60
Off hys gentrice, and off hys gudlye grace,
For yair fupple, to cunfaill gud Wallace
To cum agayn, and bring yaim off bandoun,
And tak to wer ye croun off yat regioun.
Yis wrytt as yan he wald nocht till hym fchaw,   65
Rycht laith he war for frendfchip, feid, or aw,
Wallace fuld pafs fa fone fra hys prefens,
To duelling-place he tuk to refidens.
In Schynnown ftill Wallace hys duellyng maid,
And held about rycht likand lands braid.   70

A

A keyn Captayne yan clemyt in heretage
Office off it, and gret lands in wage,
Yarfor he thocht gud Wallace for to fla.
Undyr colour fic maiftry for to ma.
Lang tyme he focht to get a day and place,   75.
Said he defyrd in feruice to Wallace.
A tryft yai fet with faxteyn on ye fyd,
Fyffte yar by he gart in bufchment byd
Off men in armys.   Quhen he with Wallace met,
Rycht awfully he bad yaim on hym fet.   80
Na armour had Wallace men in yat place,
Bot fuerd and knyff yai bur on yaim throw grace.
Parties beyn met ner a fayr foreft fyd,
Rycht bouftoufly yis Captayne faid yat tyd,
Yat Wallace held off hys lands unrycht :   85
Rycht foberly he faid to yat Franch Knycht,
I haiff na land bot quhilk ye King gaiff me,
My lyff yarfor has beyne in jeperte.
Ye Knycht anfuerd, yi lyff zow fall forlorn,
Or ellis yat land, ye contrar quha had fuorn.   90
On bak he lap, and owt hys fuerd he drew ;
Ye bufchement brak quhen he yat takyn fchew.
Gud Wallace thocht yat mattir ftud nocht weill,
He gryppyt fone a fcherand fuerd off fteill,
And at a ftraik ye Knycht to dede he draiff,   95
About faxteyn fone lappyt all ye laiff.
Wallace and hys fa worthily yai wrocht,
Full feill yai flew yat fareft on yaim focht.
Ye Knychts broyir rycht ftalwart was and ftrang,
And thocht he fuld be wengyt or yai gang,   100.

Off

Off Wallace men fum part yai woundyn fayr.
Mowand yar was intill a medow fayr
Nyne ftout carllis, all fcherwandis to yat Knycht,
Sythis yai hynt, and ran in all yair mycht
To ye fechtars; or yai com ner yat place   105
Off yaim perfawyt rycht weill was gud Wallace.
So awfull thing, off fic he neuir faw,
Yaim to rafyft hymfelff can to yaim draw;
Into ye ftour left hys men fechtand ftill,
To meit ye carllis yat com with egyr will.   110
Ye fyrft leit draw at Wallace with hys fyth,
Delyuer he was, and heich ourlappyt fwyth,
And awkwart ftraik yat churl apon ye hed,
Derfly on ground he has hym left for ded.
Ye toyir he met, ourlap hys fyth fa keyn,   115
On ye fchuldir als ftraik hym in yat teyn,
Throch all ye coft ye nobill fuerd doun fchar.
Ye thrid he met with a rycht awfull fayr
Ye groundyn fyth at Wallace he leit draw.
Yis gud Chyftane cleynly ourlap yaim aw.   120
With hys gud fuerd he maid a hidwyfs wound,
Left yaim for dede, fyne on ye ferd can found,
On ye wan bayn with gret ire can hym ta,
Cleyffyt ye coft rycht cruelly in twa.
Thre formaft fythis yus gud Wallace ourlap,   125
And four he flew, yai faw fic was hys hap;
A man he flew ay at a ftraik,
Ye laiff fled faft, yus can ye power flaik.
Wallace folowed and fone ye fyrft ourtais,
Straik hym to ded, yat na furthyr he gais,   130

Syn

Syn fped hym faft till hys awne men again,
Be yan yai had ye Knychts broyir flayn.
Sexte and fax faxteyn to ded has dycht,
Bot faiff fewyn men at fled out ofi yair fycht;
Fyffc Mclwaris yat Wallace feiff with met.   135
To Franch men fyn na fic tryfts he fet,
Becaufs yat yai hym brocht to fic a cace.
Ye King hard tell weill chapyt was Wallace,
Send for hym fone, and prayit hym for to be
Off hys houfhald, fo leyff in gud faufte;   140
For weill he faw yai had hym at inwye,
Still with hymfelff he gert hym byd for yi.
Twa zeis yus with myrth Wallace abaid
Still inte France. and mony gud jornay maid.
Ye King hyn pleffed in all hys gudly meyn,   145
Fra hyrm he fuld nocht part agayn.
Lordis and Ladys honoryd hym reuerently,
Wrechis and fchrewis ay had hym at inwy.
Twa campiowns yat tyme duelt with ye King,
Had gret defpyt at Waliace in all thing.   150
Togyddyr ay zeid yir twa campiouns,
Off felloune force and frawart attentiouns,
Rycht gret difpyt yai fpak offt off Scotland;
Quhill on a day it hapnyt apon hand,
Wallace and yai was lewyt all yaim allayn,   155
Be awentur, intill a houfs off ftayne.
Yai oyfyt to ber na wappynys in yat hall,
Yai trowyt yarfor a myfs yai mycht not fall;
Yar commound yai off Scotland fcornfully.
Yan Wallace faid yow wrang us outragely,   160.

Sen

Sen we ar bownd in frendfchipe to your King,
And he off us is pleffed in all thing ;
Als Scottfmen has helpyt yis realm off dreid,
Me think ze fuld geyff gud word for gud deid.
Qnhat may fpek off zour enemyfs bot ill?   165
In lychtlynes yai maid anfuer hym till,
And hym dyfpyt in yair langage als,
Ze Scotts, yai faid, has euir zeit beyn fals.
Wallace tuk ane on ye face in hys teyn
With hys gud hand, quhill nefs, mowth and eyn,
Throuch ye braith biaw, all byrftyt out off mud,
Butlefs to ground he fmat hym quhar he ftud.
Ye toyir hynt to Wallace in yat fteid,
For weyll he wend hys falow had beyn ded.
And he agayn in greiff hym gryppyt fayr   175
Quhill fpreits failzed ner, he mycht do na mayr.
Ye fyrft frek raifs, and fmat on Wallace faft,
Bathe to ye ded he brocht yaim at ye laft.
Apon a pyllar yair harnes out he dang,
Bot with hys hands fyn out at ye dur yaim flang, 180
And faid, quhat dewyll mowyt zon churllys at me,
Lang tyme in France I wald haiff lattyn yaim be.
Traitts for trewth yus war yai ded in deid,
Yocht Franchmen likis it nocht to reid.
Als I will cefs and put it not in rym.   185
Bettir yat is quha rycht can luk ye tym.
Mony gret Lord was difpleffyt in France,
Bot ye gud King yat knew all haill ye chance,
Oft gret difpyt off Scotland fpokyn had yai.
Yis paffit our; quhill eftir anoyir day   190
                                                     Was

Was nayn off yaim yat durſt it undirtak
He had done wrang, nor yarfor battaill mak.
Yis Ryoll Roy a hie worſchip hym gaiff;
As conquerour hym honouryd our ye laiff.
A fell Lyoun ye King has gert be brocht   195
Within a barrace, for gret harm he wrocht,
Ferlyſt in yrn, na mar power hym gaiff,
Off wodneſs he excedyt all ye laiff;
Bot he was far, and rycht felloune in deid,
In yat ſtrang ſtrenth ye King gert men hym feid,   200
Kepyt hym cloſs fra folk and beſtiall.
In ye court duelt twa ſquiers off gret waill,
At cuſyngs war on to yir campiouns twa,
Ye quhilk befor Wal'ace hapnyt to ſla.
A band yai maid in priwa illuſioun,   205
At yair power to wyrk yis confuſioun,
Be ony meyn, throw frawd or ſutelte,
Eſtir, yarfor, yai roucht not for to de,
To ded or ſchaym ſa yat yai mycht hym bryng.
Apon a tym yai went on to ye King;   210
Yis man, yai ſaid, at ze ſa weſthfull mak,
He is nocht her but he wald undyrtak,
Be hys gret fers to put to confuſioun;
Now he defyris to fecht on your Lyoun
And bad us aſk at yow yis battaill ſtrang,   215
Ze grant hym leyff in yat barrace to gang.
Sadly agayn to yaim anſuerd ye King,
Sayr me forthinkis at he defyr ſic thing;
Bot I will neuir for greyff, nor gret pleſance,
Deny Wallace quhat he deſyrs off France.   220

                        Yan

Yan went yai furth and fone met with Wallace,
A fygourd taill yai tald hym off yis cace.
Wallace, yai faid, ye King defirs yat ze
Doren battaill fa cruell be to fe,
And charges zow to fecht on hys Lyoun.   225
Wallace anfuerd in haifty conclufioun,
And faid, I fall, quhat be ye Kings will,
At my power rycht glaidly to fullfill.
Yan paffit he onto ye King but mar,
A Lord off court quhen he approchyt yar,   230
Unwyftily fperd, withoutyn prouifioun,
Wallace, dar ze go fecht on our Lyoun?
And he faid, za, fa ye King fuffyr me,
Or on yourfelff, gyff ze ocht bettyr be.
Quhat will ze mar? yis thing amityt was,   235
Yat Wallace fuld on to ye Lyoun pafs.
Ye King yarin chargyt to bring hym gud harnas;
And he faid, nay, God fcheild me fra fic cafs.
I wald tak weid, fuld I fecht with a man,
Bot a dog, yat nocht off armes can,   240
I will haiff nayn, bot fynglar as I ga;
A gret manteill about hys hand can ta,
And hys gud fuerd, with hym he tuk na mar,
Abandounly in barrace entryt yar.
Gret chemys was wrocht in ye zet with a Gyn,   245
And puld it to quhen Wallace was yarin.
Ye wode Lyoun, on Wallace quhar he ftud,
Rampand, he braid, for he defyryt blud;
With hys rude powis in ye mantill rocht fa.
Awkwart ye bak yan Wallace can hym ta   250

With hys gud fuerd yat was off burnyft fteill,
Hys body in twa it thrufchyt euyir ilk deill;
Syn to ye King he rakyt in gret ire,
And faid on loud, was yis all your defyr,
To wayr a Scott yus lychtly into wayn?   255
Is yar ma doggs at ze wald zeit haiff flayn?
Go, bryng yaim furth, fen I mon doggs qwell,
To de byddyng quhill yat I with zow duell.
It gaynd full weill I graithit me to Scotland,
For grettar deids yair men has apon hand,   260
Yan with a dog in battaill to efcheiff;
At zow in France for euir I tak my leiff.
Ye King perfawit yat Wallace grewyt was,
So ernyftfully he afkyt leiff to pafs,
Rewid in hys mynd at it was hapnyt fa,   265
Sa lewd a deid to lat hym undirta.
Knawand ye worfchip, and gret nobilnace
Off hym, quhilk fprang yat tym in mony place,
Humblely he faid, ze fuld difplefs yow nocht,
Yis ze defyryt, it mowit ner in my thocht;   270
And, be ye faith I aw ye croun off France,
I thocht neuyr to charge with fic chance,
Bot men off waill at afkyt it for yow.
Wallace anfuerd, yat God I mak a wow,
I likyt neuir fic battaill to be in,   275
Apon a dog na worfchip is to wyn.
Ye King confawyt how yis falfheid was wrocht,
Ye fquiers bath was till hys prefens brocht,
Coud nocht deny quhen yai com hym befor,
All yair trefpas yai tauld withoutyn mor.   280

Ye

Ye King commaundyt yai fuld be don to ded,
Smat off yair hedys without ony ramed.
Ye campiouns, lo, for inwy cauflace,
To fodand dede Wallace brocht yaim throw cace;
Ye fquiers als fra yair falfheid was kend,   285
Inwy yaim brocht bathe till a fodand end.
Lords, behald, inwy ye uyle dragoun,
In cruell for he burnys yis regioun;
For he is nocht, yat bond is in inwy,
To fum myfcheiff it bryngs hym haifly.   290
Forfaik inwy, yow fall ye bettir fpeid,
Heroff as now I will na fury'r reid;
Bot in my mattir, as I off for began,
I fall conteyn als playnly as I can.
Quhen Wallace faw yai had hym at inwy,   295
Langar to byd he cowd yan nocht apply,
Bettir hym thocht in Scotland for to be,
And awentur tak oyir to leiff or de,
To help hys awn he had a mar plefance,
Yan yar to byd with all ye welth off France.   300
Yus hys haill mynd, manheid and hie curage,
Was playnly fet to wyn off bondage,
Scotland agayn fra payn and felloune for,
He woude he fuld, or ellis de yarfor.
Ye King has feyn how gud Wallace was fet,   305
Ye letter yan hym gaiff withoutyn let,
Ye quhilk off lait fra Scotland was hym fend.
Wallace it faw, and weill yair harmes kend;
Be ye fyrft writ yarto accordiall,
Yaim to fupple he thocht he wald nocht faill.   310

E 2   Quhatt·

Quharto fuld I her off lang procefs mak?
Wallace off France a gudly leiff can tak.
Ye King has feyn, it wald nocht ellis be,
To chawmyr went and mycht not on hym fe,
Gret languor tuk quhen Wallace can ramuff,   315
Yat King till hym kepyt kyndnes and luff.
Jowallis and gold, hys worfchip for to faiff,
He bad yaim geyff, as much as he wald haiff.
Lordys and Ladyis wepyt wondyr faft,
Quhen Wallace yar fo tuk hys leiff, and paft.   320
No man he tuk bot quhilk he hyddyr brocht,
Agayn with hym gud Langaweill furth focht;
For payn nor blyfs yat gud Knycht left hym neuir,
Tor cace befell, quhill ded maid yaim difeuyr.
Towart ye fluce a gudly fer paft he,   325
A wefchell gat, and maid hym to ye fe,
Aucht fchipmen feit, and gudly wage yaim gaiff,
To Scotland fur, ye Fyrth off Tay yai haiff.
Apon a nycht Wallace ye land has tane
At Ernefs-mouth, and is to Elchok gane.   330
He gert ye fchip in cowert faill away,
So out off fycht yai war or it was day.
At Elchok duelt ane Wallace cufyng der,
At Crawfurd hecht; quhen yai ye houfs com ner,
On ye bakfyde Wallace a window fand,   335
And in he cald. Sone Crawfurd com at hand,
Fra tym he wyft yat it was gud Wallace,
Intill hys bern he ordand yaim a place,
A mow off corn he guhyt yaim about,
And clofyt weill, nane mycht perfaive without;   340

                                                                                Bot

Bot at a place quhar meit he to yaim brocht,

As bedyn to als glaidly as he mocht,

A dern holl furth, on ye north fyd, yai had

To ye wattir, quharoff Wallace was glad.

Four dayis or fyffe in reft yai foiornd yar,   345

Quhill meit was gayn, yan Crawfurd bound for mar

Till Santt Jhonftoun, yair purweance for to by.

Inglifmen thocht he tuk mar boundandly

Yan he was wount at any tym befor;

Yai haiff hym tane, put hym in prefoune for,   350

Quhat gefts he had, to tell yai mak raqueft.

He faid, it was bot till a kyrkyn feft;

Zeit yai preiff fone ye cumyng off Wallace,

Knawlage to get yai keft a futtell cace.

Yai lat hym pafs with thing yat he had bocht,   355

Syn eftir fone in all ye haift yai mocht

To harnes zeid ye power off ye toun.

Aucht hundreth men with Butler maid yaim boun,

Folowed on dreich, quhill at yis man cum hame.

Wallace hym faw, and faid, he ferwyt blame.   360

In my flepyng a full vifioun me tauld,

Till Inglifmen yat yow fuld me haiff fauld.

Crawfurd hym faid, he had beyn turment fayr

With Inglifmen, yat had hym in difpayr;

Yarfor ryfs up, and for fum fuccour fe,   365

I dreid full fayr, yai fet wachis on me.

Ye worthi Scotts yai graithit yaim in gud weid,

Yair wappynys tuk, fyn off yat houfs furth zeid.

Yus fedandly ye fell Sothroune yai faw,

To few yai war to bid agayn yaim aw,   370

At keynly com with zoung Butler ye Knycht.
Yan Wallace faid, a playn fcild is not rycht,
Bot Elchok park is ner hand her befyd,
Ye fyrft failzie we think yar to byd.
Nyneteyn yai war, and Crawfurd, with gud will,   375
Ye twentyd man, ye nowmir to fullfill.
Ye park yai tuk, Wallace a place has feyn
Off gret holyns, yat grew bath heich and greyn,
With thuortour treis a mannir ftrenth maid he,
Or yat war wone yai trowyt to gar feill de.   380
Ye wode was theyk, bot litill off breid or buth,
Had yai had meit, yai thocht to hald yat ftrenth.
Ye Inglifmen paffyt to Crawfurdis place,
Fand in ye bern ye lugyng off Wallace ;
Yan Crafurdis wyff in handis haiff yai tane,   385
And aft at hyr quhat way ye Scotts war gane ;
Rycht weill yai trowit at Wallace fuld yar be,
Off France in Tay he was cummyn be ye fe.
Sche wald nocht tell, for boft, nor zeit reward.
Yan Butler faid, our lang yow has beyn fpard ;   390
Yarwith he grew in mattelent and ire,
And gert yaim byg a baillfull braid brym fyr,
Ye Sothroune fuor yarin fche fuld brynt be.
Yan Wallace faid, fche fall not end for me ;
Gret fyn it war zon faiklefs wycht to fla.   395
Or fche fuld end, in faith yar fall de ma.
He left ye ftrenth, and ye playn fcild can ta,
On lowd he cryit, and faid, lo, her I ga.
Thinkis yow no fchaym for to turment a wyff,
Cum fyrft to me and mak end off our ftryff.   400

                                                 Fra

Fra Butlar had apon gud Wallace feyn,
Throuch auld malice he wox ner wod for teyn,
Apon ye Scotts fchup yaim all with gret mayn,
Bot Wallace fone ye ftrenth he tuk agayn.
A fell bykkyr ye Inglifmen began,　　　　　405
Affailzied fayr with mony cruell man;
Bot yai within war nobiil at defens,
Maid gret debait be force and wiolence.
At ye entre fyffteyn yai brocht to ded,
Yan all ye laive ramowyt fra yat fted,　　　410
Zeid till aray agayn to failze new.
Wallace beheld quhilk weill in wer hym knew,
Falowis, he faid, agayn all at yis place
Yai wiil nocht faill, but yus ftandis ye cace.
Zon Knycht thinkis for to dewid hys men　　415
In feir parts ye futh ze fall weill ken,
Agayn on us to preiff how it may be;
Us worthys now fum wayis for yaim to fe,
Contrar yair rycht a gud defens to mak.
Now Longaweill, zow fall fex with ze tak,　　420
Wilzam my Eym als mony fall with zow ga,
And fyffe with me, as now we haiff na ma.
Knycht Butler yan partyt hys men in thre.
Wallace wefyd quhar Butler fchup to be,
Yiddyr he paft yat entre for to wer,　　　　425
On ilka fyd yai failze with gret fer.
Wallace leit part in ye entre begyn,
Bot nane zeid out yat on ye Scotts com in.
Sewyn formaft was quhilk in ye foreft zeid,
Wallace fyffe man quhilk douchty was in deid,　430

Ilk

Ilk ane flew ane, and Wallace gert twa de.
Butler was next, and faid, yis will nocht be,
On bak he drew, and leit hys curage flaik,
Ye worthi Scotts prowit weill for Scotlands faik,
Gud Longaweill hys cowntyr maid fo far,   435
And Crawfurd als, yai failzeid yan no mar.
Rycht ner be yan approchyt to ye nycht,
And fternys uppeyr began in to yair fycht,
Sothroune fet wach, and to yair fouper went.
Ye Butlar was fayr grewyt in hys entent,   440
Zeit fur yai weill off ftuff, wyn, ayle and breid.
Wallace and hys yai wyft off na rameid
Bot cauld wattir yan ran throuchout a ftrand,
In yat lugyng nane oyir fud yai fand.
Yan Wallace faid, gud falowis think nocht lang,   445
Will God, we fall be fone out off yis thrang,
Suppofs we faft a day, our and a nycht,
Tak all in thank yis payn for Scotlands rycht.
Ye Erle off Zork was in Santt Jhonftoune ftill,
To Butlar fend, and bad hym byd at will,   450
Till hym full fone yar fuld cum new power,
And als hymfelff, yus tald ye meffynger.
Butlar wald fayn Wallace had zeldyn beyn
Or ye Erle com, for yis cauffis was feyn,
Hys Grantfchyr bathe and hys Fadyr he flew,   455
Yis Knycht yarwith towart ye park hym drew,
Quhat cher yai maid, apon ye Scotts cald,
Yan Wallace faid, fer bettyr yan ze wald,
Ye Butlar faid, I wald fayn fpek with ze.
Wallace anfuerd, yow may for litill fe.   . 460

                                        Wallace,

Wallace, he faid, yow yas done me gret fcaith,
My rycht Fadyr and Grantfchyr yow flew baith.
Yan Wallace faid, for ftait yat yow ar in,
It war my det for till undo yi kyn.
I think als, fa God off Hewyn me faiff,   465
At my twa hands fall graith ye to yi graiff.
Ye Butlar faid, yat is nocht likly now,
In my credence, and yow will fermly trow,
Off yis I afk, and yow will mak me grant,
Quhat I ye hecht, yat thing yow fall nocht want. 470
Sa furth quoth he be yi defyr refonable
I fall it grant withoutyn ony fable.
Ye Butlar faid, Wallace, yow knawis rycht,
Yow may nocht chaip for power nor for flycht;
And fen ze feis it may nocht bettir be,   475
For yi gentrice yow will zeild ze to me.
Yan Wallace faid, yi will unfkillfull is,
Zow wald I did quhilk is our hye a myfs,
Zoldin I am to bettir, I can pruff,
To mychty God, yat makar is, abuff;   480
For euir ilk day, fen I had wyt off man,
Defor my werk, to zeild me I began;
At als at ewyn, quhen yat I failzeid lycht,
I me betuk to ye makar off mycht.
Ye Butler faid, me think yow has done weill,   485
Zeit off a thing, I pray zow, lat me feill,
For yi manheid yus furthwart to me feft
Quhen yat zow feis yow may nocht langar left
On yis ilk place, quhilk I haiff tane to wer,
Yat yow cum furth, and all oyir forber.   490

Yan

Yan Wallace leuch at hys cruell defyr,
And faid, I fall, yocht yow war wod as fyr,
And all Ingland contrar yaroff had fuorn,
I fall cum out at yat iłk place to morn,
Or ellys to nycht, traift weill quhat I ze fay,   495
I byd nocht her quhill nyn hours off ye day.
Butler fend furth ye chak wach on ilka fyd.
In yat ilk place bauldly he bownyt to byd.
Yus ftill yai baid quhill day began to peyr
A thyk myft fell, ye planet was nocht cler.   500
Wallace affayed at all place about,
Leit as he wald at ony place brek out ;
Quhill Butlers men fum part fra hym can ga
To help ye laive quhen yai faw it was fa.
Wallace and hys faft fped yaim to yat fted   505
Quhar Butlar baid, feill men yai draiff to ded,
Ye worthi Scotts fone paft throuch yat melle,
Crawfurd yair oyft was fayr hurt on ye kne,
At erd he was, gud Wallace turnd agayn,
And at a ftraik he has ye Butlar flayn,   510
Hynt up yat man undyr hys arm fa ftrang,
Defendand hym out off yat felloune thrang.
Gud rowm he maid amang yaim quhar he gais,
With hys rycht hand he flew fyffe off yair fais ;
Bur furth Crawfurd, be force off hys perfoun,   515
Nyne akyr breid, or euir he fet hym doun.
Ye Sothroune fand at yair Captayne was ded,
All hym about, bot yan was no rameid ;
Threty with hym off ye wychtaft yai brocht,
Ded at yat place quhar as ye Scotts furth focht.   520

                                        Wallace

Wallace and hys be yan was off yair fycht,
Sothroune baid ftill for for lofs off yat Knycht.
Ye myft was myrk, yat Wallace lis it weill,
Hymfelff was gyd, and faid to Langaweill,
At Meffan-wode is my defyr to be,   525
On beftiall yarfor meit yat we may fe.
Be yan yai war weill cumyn to ye hycht,
Ye myft fealyt, ye fone fchawit fayr and brycht;
Son war yai war, a litill fpace yaim by
Tour and twenty was in a cumpany.   530
Yan Wallace faid, be zon men freynd or fa,
We will to yaim, fen at yai ar na ma.
Quhen yai com ner, a nobill Knycht it was,
Ye quhilk to name hecht Elyfs off Dundafs,
And Schyr Jhon Scot ek, a worthi Knycht,   535
Into Straithern a man off mekill mycht;
For yar he had gret part off heretage,
Dundafs fyftyr he had in mariage.
Paffand yai war, and mycht no langar left,
Till Inglifmen, yair fewte for to teft.   540
Lord off Breichyn fic connand had yaim maid,
Off Edwarde yai fuld bald yair Landys braid;
Bot fra yai faw yat it was wycht Wallace,
Leyftyt yair handis, and thankit God off Grace,
Off hys gret help quhilk he had fend yaim yar.   545
To Meffen-wode with ane affent yai far,
Sone gat yaim meit and beftiall at yai fand,
Reftyt yat day, quhen nycht was cumyn on hand,
To Byrnam-wode, but reftyng, ar yai gayne,
Quhar yai found ye fquier gud Ruwayn,   550

In

In outlaw oyfs he had lang lewyt yair
On beftiall, quhill he mycht get na mair.
Yai taryt nocht, bot intill Adell zeid,
Quhar meit was fcant, yan Wallace had gret dreid,
Paft intill Lorn, and rycht litill fand yair,   555
Off wyld and taym yat contre was maid bair;
Bot in ftrenthis, yar fud was lewyt nayn,
Ye worthi Scotts yan maid a petoufs mayn.
Schyr Jhon Scott faid, he had fer leuir de
Intill gud naym, and leyff hys ayrs fre,   560
Yan for till byd as bond in fubiectioun.
Quhen Wallace faw yir gud men off renoun
With hungyr ftad, almaft mycht leyff no mar,
Wyt ze, for yaim he fichit wondyr far.
Gud men, he faid, I am ye caufs off yis,   565
At zour defyr I fall amend yis wyfs,
Or leiff zow fre fum chewyfians to ma,
All hym allayn he bownyt fra yaim to ga;
Prayit yaim to byd quhill he mycht com agayn,
Atour a hill he paffit till a playn.   570
Out off yair fycht intill a foreft fyd,
He fat hym doun undyr ane ayk to byd;
Hys bow and fuerd he lenyt till a tre,
In angwyfs greiff, on grouff fo turned he,
Hys petous mynd was for hys men fa wrocht,   575
Yat off hymfelff litill as yan he rocht.
O wrech! he faid, yat neuir couth be content
Off our gret mycht, yat ye Gret God ye lent,
Bot yi fers mynd willfull and wariable,
With gret Lordfchip yow coud nocht fo byd ftable; 580
And

And willfull witt, for to mak Scotland fre,
God likis nocht yat I haiff tane on me,
For worthyar off bryth yan I was born,
Throuch my defyr, with hungyr ar lorn.
I afk at God yaim to refter agayn,   585
I am ye caufs I fuld haiff all ye payn.
Quhill ftudeand yus, quhill flytand with hymfell,
Quhill at ye laft apon a flepyng he fell.
Thre dayis befor yar had hym folowed fyffe,
Ye quhilk was bound, or ellis to lofs yair lyffe;   590
Ye Erle off Zork bad yaim fo gret gardoun,
At yai be thyft hecht to put Wallace doun.
Thre off yaim was all born men off Ingland,
And twa was Scotts, yat tuk yis deid on hand ;
And fum men faid, yair thrid broyir betraiffed   595
Kyldrome eft, quhar gret forow was raiffed.
A child yai bad, quhilk helpyt to ber meit
In wyldernes amang ye montans gret.
Yai had all feyn diffeuyryng off Wallace
Fra hys gud men, and quhar he baid on cace,   600
Amang thik wode in couert held yaim law,
Quhill yai perfawyt he was on flepyng faw,
And yan yir fyffe apprechit Wallace ner,
Quhat beft to do at oyir can yai fpeir.
A man faid yus, it war a hie renoun,   605
And we mycht quyk leid hym to Santt Jhonftoun ;
Lo, how he lyis, we may our gryppys waill,
Off hys wappynys he fall get nane awaill,
We fall hym bynd in contrar off hys will,
And leid hym yus on bakfyd off zon hill,   610

So yat hys men fall nothing off hẏm knaw
Ye toyir four aſſentyt till hys faw;
And yan yir fyffe maid yaim to Wallace,
And thocht throw force to bynd hym in yat place.
Quhat, trowit yir fyffe for to hald Wallace doun, 615
Ye manlyaſt man, ye ſtarkaſt off perſoun
Leyffand he was, and als ſtud in ſic rycht,
We traiſt weill, God hys deds had in ſycht.
Yai gryppyt hym, yan out off ſlepe he braid,
Quhat menys yis rycht ſedandly he ſaid.   620
About he turnyt, and up hys armys thrang,
On yai tratours with Knycht-lik fers he dang,
Ye ſtarkaſt man untill hys armys hynt he,
And all hys harnys he dang out on a tre;
A ſuerd he gat ſone eftyr yat he raiſs,   625
Campioun-lik amang ye four he gais,
Euyr a man he gert de at a dynt,
Quhen twa was ded, ye toyir was nocht ſtynt,
Maid yaim to fle, bot yan it was na but,
Was nane leyffand mycht paſs fra hym on fut.   630
He folowed faſt, and ſone to ded yaim brocht,
Yan to ye chyld ſadly agayn he ſocht.
Quhat did zow her? Ye chyld, with paill face,
On kneis he fell, and aſkyt Wallace grace,
With yaim I was, and knew na thing yair thocht, 635
Into ſchyruice, as yai me bad, I wrocht:
Quhat berys yow her? Bot meit, ye chyld can ſay.
Do, turſs it up, and paſs with me away.
Meit in yis tym is fer bettyr yan gold.
Wallace and he furth foundyt our ye fold,   640

Quha

Quha broucht Wallace fra hys enemyfs bauld,
Quhat bot Gret God yat has ye warld in wauld,
He was hys help in mony felloune thrang,
With glaid cheyr yus on till hys men can gang.
Bathe roftyt flefche yar was, als breid and cheis. 645
To fuccour yaim yat was in poynt to leis;
Yan he it delt to four men and fyfte,
Quhilk had befor faftyt our dayis thre,
Syn tuk hys part, he had faft yt als lang.
Quhar herd ze euir ony in fic a thrang,   650
In hungyr fo flepand, and wapynlafs,
So weill recouer as Wallace did yis cafs?
Playnly be fors vencuft hys enemyfs fyive.
Ze men off witt yis queftioun dyfcryive
Withoutyn gloifs, I will tell furth my taill.   655
How com yis meit? Ye falowfchip afkyt haill.
To yar defyr Wallace nane anfuer zald,
Quhar fyffe war ded he led yaim furth, fyne tald.
Gretly difpleffyd was all yat chewalry,
Till a Chyftane, yai held it fantafy,   660
To walk allayn.   Wallace, with fobyr mind,
Said, as heroff is nothing cummyn bot gud.
To ye law land full faft agayn yai focht,
Sperd at yis chyld gyff he couth wyfs yaim ocht,
Quhar yai mycht beft off purweance for to wyn. 665
Off nane he faid was yat contre within,
Nor all about, as fer as I can knaw,
Quhill yat yow com doun to ye Ranoucht-haw,
Yat Lord has ftuff, breid, all and gud warnage,
Off King Edwarde he takis full mekill wage.   670

Yan Wallace faid, myfelff fall be zour gyd,
I knaw yat fted about on ayir fyd.
Throuch ye wyld land he gydyt yaim full rycht,
To Ranouch-hall yai com apon ye nycht.
A wach was out, and yat full fone yai ta,   675
For he was Scotts, yat man yai wald nocht fla,
Bot gart hym tell ye manner off yat place;
Yus entryt yai within a litill fpace.
Ye zet yai wan, for caftell was yar nayn,
Bot mud-wall werk withoutyn lym or ftayn.   680
Wallace in haift ftraik up ye chawmir-dur
Bot with hys fut, yat ftalwart was and ftur.
Yan yai within fa walknyt fodeynly,
Ye Lord gat up, and mercy can he cry;
Fra tym he wyft yat gud Wallace was yar,   685
He thankyt God, fyn faid yir words mar,
Trow man I was, and woun agayn my will
With Inglifmen, fuppofs I likit ill.
All Scotts we ar yat in yis place is now,
At your commaund a'l playnly fall we bow.   690
Off our natioun gud Wallace had pete.
Tuk aythis off yaim, fyne meit afkyt he.
Gud cheyr yai maid quhill lycht day on ye morn.
Yis trew man yan fone femblyt hym beforn
Thre fonnys he had, yat ftalwart war and bauld, 695
And twentye men off hys kyn in houfhauld.
Wallace was blyth yai maid hym fic fupple,
Said, I thank God, yat we yus multiple.
All yat day our in gud liking yai reft,
Wachys yai waill to kep yaim at coud beft,   700

Apon

Apon ye morn ye lycht day quhen yai faw,
Yan Wallace faid, our power for to knaw,
We will tak feild, and up our baner raifs
Off rycht Scotland, in contrar off our fais.
We will no mar now us in cowert hyd,   705
Power till us will fembill on ilk fyd.
Horfs yai gat, ye beft men at was yar,
Towart Dunkell ye gayneft way yai far.
Ye Byfchop fled, and gat to Santt Jhonftoun,
Ye Scotts flew all was yar off yat natioun,   710
Bathe pur and rych, and fcherwandis at yai fand,
Left nane on lyff yat born was off Ingland.
Ye place yai tuk, and maid yaim weill to fayr,
Off purweance yat Byfchop had brocht yair.
Jowllys yai gat, bath gold and filuer brycht,   715
With gud cheyr yar fyffe dayis yai foiornyt rycht ;
On ye fext day Wallace to confaill went,
Gert call ye beft, and fchew yaim hys entent.
Na men we haiff to failze Santt Jhenftoun,
In to ye north yarfor lat mak us boun.   720
In Rofs, yow knaw, gud men a ftrenth has maid,
Her yai off us, yai com withoutyn baid ;
Als into But ye Byfchop gud Synclar,
Fra he get wyt, he will com withoutyn mar.
Gud weftland men off Aran and Rauchle,   725
Fra yai be warnd, yai will all com to me.
Yis purpofs tuk, and in ye north yai rid,
Nan Inglifmen durft in yair way abid.
Quham Wallace tuk, yai knew ye ald ranfoun,
Fra he com laym, to fle yai mak yaim boun,   730

F 3   And.

And Scotts men femblyt to Wallace faft,
In awfull feyr throuchout ye land yai paft.
Strenthis was left, witt ye, all defolate,
Agayn yir folk yai durft mak no debate.
In rayit battaill yai raid till Abyrdeyn,   735
Ye haill nowmyr, fewyn thoufand yan was feyn;
Bot Inglifmen had left yat toun all waift,
On ilka fyd away yai can yaim haift,
In all yat land left noyir mar nor lefs.
Lord Bewmond tuk ye fey at Bowchannefs.   742
Throuch Scotland yan was manyfeft in playn,
Ye Lords yat paft in harts war wondyr fayn.
Ye Knycht Climes off Rofs com fodeynly
In Murray land with yair gud chewalry.
Ye houfs off Narn yat gud Knycht weill has tane, 745
Slew ye Captayne and ftrang men mony aue;
Owt off Murray in Bowchan land com yai
To fek Bewmound, be he was paft away;
Yan yir gud men to Wallace paffit rycht.
Quhen Wallace faw Schyr Jhon Ramfay ye Knycht,
And oyir gud at had bene fra hym lang,
Gret curage yan was raffyt yaim amang.
Ye land he rewllyt as at hym lykyt beft
To Santt Jhonftoun fyn raid or yai wald reft.
At cuir ilk part a ftalwart wach he maid,   755
Fermyt a fege and ftedfaftly abaid,
Byfchop Synclar into all haift hym dycht,
Com out off But with fymly men to fycht;
Out off ye Ilys off Rauchle and Aran,
Lyndfay and Boid, with gud men mony ane,   760

Adam

Adam Wallace Barroun off Ricardtoun
Full fadly focht till Wallace off renoun.
Off Santt Jhonftoun baid at ye failze ftill,
For Sothroune men yai mycht weill pafs at will;
For in yair way yar durft na enemys be,   765
Bot fled away be land, and als be fe.
About yat toun yus femblyt yai but mar,
For yai had beyn with gud Wallace befor.
Cetoun, Lawdir, and Richard off Lunde,
In a gud barge yai paft about be fe;   770
Santt Jhonftons-toun hawyn yair ankyr haiff yai fet.
Twa Inglis fchippys yai tuk withoutyn let,
Ye tane yai brynt, fyne ftuffyt ye toyir weill
With artailze, and ftalwart men in fteill,
To kep ye port, yar fuld com na wittaill   775
Into yat toun, nor men at mycht yaim waill.
Fra fouth and north mony off Ingland fled,
Left caftellys waift, feill left yar lyff to wed.
Ye South Byfchope befor yat left Dunkell,
Till London paft, and tald Edwarde hymfell,   780
In Scotland yar had fallyn a gret myfchance.
Yan fend he fone for Amar ye Wallance,
And afkyt hym yan quhat war beft to do.
He hecht to pafs, and tak gret gold yarto,
Into Scotland, fic monys for to mak,   785
Agayn Wallace on hand yis can he tak.
Yai faid, he wald undo King Edwards croun,
Bot gyff yai mycht throuch trefoun put hym doun.
King Edward hecht, quhat thing at Wallang band,
He fuld it kepe, war it bath gold and land.   790

                   Wallang

Wallang tuk leyff, and is in Scotland went,
To Bothwell com, fyn keft in hys entent.
Quhat man yar was mycht beft Wallace begyll,
And fone he fand, within a litill quhill,
Schyr Jhon Menteth, Wallace hys goffep was.   795
A meffynger Schyr Amar has gart pafs
On to Schyr Jhon, and fone a tryft has fet,
At Ruglan Kyrk yir twa togydder met.
Yan Wallang faid, Schyr Jhon yow knaw yis thing,
Wallace agayn ryffys contrar ye King,   800
And yow may haiff quhat Lordfchip yow will waill!
And yow wald wyrk as I can gyff cunfaill.
Zon tyrand haldys ye realmys at troubill bath,
Till thryfty men it dois full mckill fcaith.
He traifts ye, rycht weill yow may hym tak,   805
Off yis mater ane end I think to mak.
War he away, we mycht at lyking ryng
As Lordys all, and leyff undyr a King.
Yan Menteth faid, he is our Gouernour,
For us he baid in mony felloune ftour,   810
Nocht for hymfelff, bot for our heretage;
To fell hym yus it war a foull owtrage.
Yan Wallang faid, and yow weill undyrftud,
Cret neid it war, he fpillis fo mekill blud
Off Cryftin men, putts faullis in perell;   815
I bynd me als, he fall be haldyn haill,
As for hys lyff, and kepyt in prefoun;
King Edwarde wald haiff hym in fubjectioun.
Yan Menteth, fa wald kep connand,
He wald full fayn had hym in Scotland.   820

Wallang

Wallang faw hym intill a ftudy be,
Thre thoufand poundys off fyn gold lat hym fe,
And hecht he fuld ye Lewyn-houfs haiff at will.
Yus trefonably Menteth grantyt yartill ;   •
Obligatioun with hys awn hand he maid,   825
Syn tuk ye gold, and Edwards feill fo braid,
And gaiff yaim hys, quhen he hys tym mycht fe
To tak Wallace our Sulway, giff hym fre
Till Inglifmen ; be yis trefonabill concord
Schyr Jhon fuld be off all ye Lennox Lord.   830
Yus Wallace fuld in Ingland kepyt be,
So Edwarde mycht mak Scotland till hym fre.
Yair cowatyfs was our gret mayftir feyn,
Nane fampill taks how ane oyir has beyne.
For cowatyfs, put in gret paynys fell   835
For cowatyfs, ye ferpent is off hell.
Throuch cowatyfs, gud Ectour to ye ded
For cowatyfs, yar can be na ramed.
Throw cowatyfs gud Alexander was loft,
And Julius als for all hys reyff and boft.   840
Throuch cowatyf deit, Arthour off Bretan.
For cowatyfs, yar had deid mony ane.
For cowatyfs, ye traytour Ganzelon
Ye flour off France he put till confufioun.
For cowatyfs yai poyfound gud Godfra   845
In Antioche, as ye autor will fa.
For cowatyfs, Menteth, apon falfs wyfs,
Betrayfyt Wallace yat was hys goffop twyfs,
Wallang in haift, with blyth will and glaid hart.
Till London paft, and fchawit King Edwart.   850

                                                     Of

Off yis contrak and had a mar plefance,
Yan off fyn gold had geyffyn in ballance.
A grettar wecht na hys ranfoun mycht be,
Off Wallace furth fum thing fpek will we.
At Santt Jhonftoune was at ye fegyng ftill.   855
In a mornyng Sothroune with egyr will,
Fyffe hundreth men in harnas rycht juntly,
Yai ufchyt furth to mak a jeperte
At ye fouth part, apon Scott and Dundafs,
Quhilk in yat tym rycht wyfs and worthi was,   860
Agayn yair fayis rycht fcharply focht and fayr,
In yat cowntyr fewyn fcor to ded yai bayr.
Zeit Inglifmen, at cruell war and keyn,
Full ferfly faucht, quhar douchty deid was feyn,
Fra ye weft zet drew all ye Scotts haill   865
To ye fechtars.   Quhen Sothroune faw no waill,
Bot in agayn full faft yai can yaim fped,
Ye Knycht Dundafs prowyt fa douchty deid.
Our ner ye zett fo bandounly he baid,
With a gud fuerd full gret maftry he maid;   870
Nocht wittandly hys falowis was hym fra,
In at ye zett ye Sothroune can hym ta,
On to ye Erle yai led hym haiftele.
Quhen he hym faw, he faid he fuld nocht de;
To flay yis ane it may us litill ramcid;   875
He fend hym furth to Wallace in yat fteid.
On ye north fyd hys beftialls had he wrocht,
Quhill he hym faw, off yis he wyft rycht nocht,
Send to ye Erle, and thankyt hym largele,
Hecht for to quyt quhen he fic cace mycht fe;   880

Bot

But all herfor fouerance he wald nocht grant,
Zocht yai goldin wald com at recreant ;
For gold na gud, he wald na treubut tak,
A full ſtrang ſalt yan he begouth to mak.
Ye Erle off Fyff duelt undyr trewage lang   885
Off King Edwarde, and yan hym thocht it wrang,
At Wallace ſa was ſegeand Sant Jhonſtoun,
But gyff he com in rycht help off ye croun.
Till Inglifmen he wald nocht kep yat band,
Yan he com fone with gud men off ye land ;   890
And Jhon Wallang was yan Schyrreſſ off Fyff,
Till Wallace paſt, ſtarkyt hym in yat ſtryſſ.
Yat Erle was cummyn off trew haill nobill blud,
Fra ye ald Thane, quhilk in hys tym was gud.
Yan all about to Santt Jhonſtoun yai gang,   895
With felloune ſalt was hydwyſs ſcharp and ſtrang,
Full feill fagaldys into ye dyk yai caſt,
Hadyr and hay bond apon ſtakys faſt,
With treis and erd a gret paſſage yai maid,
Atour ye wallis yai zeid with battaill braid.   900
Ye Sothroune men maid gret defens agayn,
Quhill on ye wallys yar was a thouſand ſlayn.
Wallace zeid in and hys rayit battaill rycht,
All Sothroune men derfly to ded yai dycht.
To ſaiff ye Erle Wallace ye harrold ſend,   905
Gud Jop hymſelff, ye quhilk befor hym kend ;
For Dundaſs ſaik yai ſaid he ſuld nocht de,
Wallace hymſelff yus ordand for to be.
A ſmall haknay he gert till hym betak,
Siluer and gold hys coſts for to mak,   910

Set

Set on hys clok a takyn for to se,
Ye Lyoun in Wax yat suld hys condet be,
Conwoyit hym furth, and na man hym withall,
Wemen and barnys Wallace gert freich yaim all,
And fyn gert cry, trew Scottsmen to yair awn,   915
Plenyst ye land quhilk lang had beyn ourthrawn.
Yan Wallace past ye southland for to se
Edward ye Bruce, in hys tym rycht worthe ;
Yat yer befor he had in Irland beyn,
And purchest yaroff cruell men and keyn: 920
Fyffty in feyr was off hys modrys keyn
At Kirkubre on Galloway entryt in ;
With yai fyffe he had vencuft nyne scor,
And fyn he paft, withoutyn tary mor,
Till Wigtoun fone, and yat Caftell has tane,   925
Sothronne was fled, and left all allane.
Wallace hym met with treu men reuerently,
To Lowchmaban went all yat chewalry.
Yai maid Edwarde bathe Lord and Ledar yar,
Yis conditioun Wallace hym hecht but mar.   930
But a fchort tym to byd Robert ye King,
Gyff he cam nocht in yis regioun to ryng,
At Edwarde fuld rafaiff ye croun but faill,
Yus hecht Wallace, and all ye barnage haill.
In Lowchmaban Prynce Edwarde lewyt ftill,   935
And Wallace paft in Cumno with blyth will,
At ye Blak Rok quhar he was wount to be,
Apon yat fted a ryoll houfs held he.
Inglis wardans till London paft but mar,
And tauld ye King off all yair gret mysfar,   940

How

How Wallace had Scotland fra yaim reduce,
And how he had refawyt Edwarde ye Bruce.
Ye commoune fuor yai fuld cum neuir mar
Apon Scotland and Wallace leiffand war.
Yan Edwarde wrayt till Menteth prewaly,   945
Prayit hym till haift, ye tym was paft by.
Off ye promefs ye quhilk at he was bund.
Schyr Jhon Menteth intill hys witt has fund,
How he fuld beft hys purpos to fulfill.
Hys fyftars fone in haift he cauld hym till,   950
And ordand hym in duellyng with Wallace;
Ane ayth agayn he gert hym mak on cace,
Quhat tym he wyft Wallace in quiet draw,
He fuld hym warn, for awentur mycht befaw.
Yis man grantyt at fic thing ful be done,   955
With Wallace yus he was in fcherwice fone.
As off trefoun Wallace had litill thocht,
Hys lawbourous mynd on oyir matters wrocht.
Yus Wallace thryfs has maid all Scotland fre,
Yan he defyryt in leftand pefs to be;   960
For as off wer he has in fum part yrk,
He purpoft yan to fcherwe God and ye kyrk,
And for to leyff undyr hys rychtwyfs King;
Yat he defyryt abowne all erdly thing.
Ye harrold Jop in Ingland fone he fend,   965
And wrait till Bruce rycht hartly hys commend,
Befekand hym to cum and tak hys croun,
Nane fuld gaynftand, Clerk, Burges, na Barroun.
Ye herrald paft, quhen Bruce faw hys credans,
Yaroff he tuk a perfyt gret plefans;   970

VOL. III.   **G**   With

With hys awn hand agayn wraitt to Wallace,
And thankyt hym off lawte and kyndnefs,
Befekand hym yis mater to confeyll,
For he behuffyd out off ngland to fteill,
For lang befor was kepyt ye Ragment,   975
Quhilk Cumyn had to byd ye gret parlement,
Into London, and gyff yai hym accufs,
To cum fra yaim he fuld mak fum excufs.
He prayit Wallace in Glafkow-mur to walk
Ye fyrft nycht off Juli for hys falk,   980
And bad he fuld bot into quiet be,
For he with hym mycht bryng few chewalre.
Wallace was glaid quhen he yis wryttyng faw,
Hys housfhald fone he gert to Glafkow draw,
Yat moneth yar he ordand hym to byd,   985
Kerle he tuk ilk nycht with hym to ryd,
And yis zong man yat Menteth till hym fend,
Wyft nane bot yir quhat way at Wallace wend;
Ye quhilk gart warn hys Eym ye auchtand nycht.
Sexte full fone Schyr Jhon gert dycht   990
Off hys awn kyn, and off Alay was born,
To yis trefoune he gert yaim all be fuorn.
Fra Dimbertane he fped yaim haiftily,
Ner Glafkow kyrk yai bownyt yaim priwaly.
Wallace paft furth quhar yat ye tryft was fet, 995
A fpy yai maid, and folowed hym but let,
Till Robraftoun was ner be ye way fyd,
And bot a houfs quhar Wallace oyffyt to byd,
He wouk on fut quhill paffit was mydnycht;
Kerly and he yan for a fleip yaim dycht.   1000

                                    Yai

Yai bad yis cuk, yat he fuld wach hys part,
Ard wakyn Wallace, com men tra ony **art.**
Quhen yai flepyt, yis traytour fuk gud heid,
Demet **hys** Fym, and bad hym haiff no dreid,
On **fleip he** is, and with hym bot a man,   1005
Ze may hym haiff, for ony craft he can,
Without ye houfs yair wappyr ys baid yaim fra,
For weill yai wyft, gat Wallace ane off ya,
And on hys feyt, hys ranfoun fuld be fauld;
Yus femblit yai about yat febill hauld.   1010
Ye traytour wach fra Wallace yan he ftaw
B:**the** knyff and fuerd, hys bow and arowis aw;
Eftyr mydnycht in hands yai haiff hym tane,
Dyfchowyll on fleip, with hym no man bot ane.
Kerle yai tuk, and led hym off yat place,   1015
Dyd hym **to** ded withoutyn langar fpace.
Yai thocht to bynd Wallace throw ftrenthis ftrang,
On fute he gat ye feill traytours amang,
Gryppyt about, bot na wapyn he fand,
Apon a tyll he faw befyd hym ftand,   1020
Ye bak off ane he byrftyt in yat thrang,
And off ane oyir ye harnefs out he dang.
Yan als mony as handis on hym mycht lay,
Be fors hym hynt for till haiff hym away;
Bot yat power mycht nocht a fute hym leid   1025
Owt off yat houfs, quhill yai or he war deid.
Schyr Jhon fa weill be fors it mycht nocht be,
Or he war tane he thocht erar to de.
Menteth bad cefs, and yus fpak to Wallace,
Syne fchawit hym furth a rycht futell fals cace.   1030

Ye haiff so lang her oyssyt zow allane,
Quhill witt yaroff is intill Ingland gane,
Yarfor her me, and fobyr zour curage.
Ye Inglifmen, with a full gret barnage,
Ar femblyt her, and fet yis houfs about,   1035
Yat ze, be fors, on na wayis may wyn out.
Suppofs yow had ye ftrenth off gud Ectour,
Amang yis oft ye may nocht lang endour,
And yai zow tak, in haift your dede is dycht.
I haiff fpokyn with Lord Clyffurd yat Knycht,   1040
With yair chyftanys weill menyt for zour lyff,
Yai afk no mar but be quyt off zour ftryff.
To Dimbertane ze fall furth pafs with me,
At zour awn houfs ze may in faufte be.
Sothroune fic oyfs with Menteth lang had yai,   1045
Yat Wallace trowit fum part yat he wald fay,
Menteth faid, fchyr, lo, wappynys nane we haiff,
We com in trayft, zour lyff gyff we mycht faiff.
Wallace trowit weill, and he hys goffop twyfs,
Yat he wald nocht, be ony maner off wyfs,   1050
Hym to betrayfs for all Scotland fo wyd,
Ane ayth off hym he afkyt in yat tyd,
Yar wantyt wytt, quhat fuld hys aythis mor,
For fuorn till hym he was lang tym befor.
Ye ayth he maid, Wallace cum in hys will,   1055
Rycht frawdfully all yis fchawit hym till.
Goffop, he faid, as prefouner yai mon yow fe,
Or yai throuch force will ellis tak yow fra me.
A courch with flycht apon hys handys yai laid,
And undyr fyne with feuar cordys yai braid,   1060

Bath

Bath fcharp and tewch, and faft togyddyr drew,
Allace ye Bruce mycht fayr yat byndyng rew,
Quhilk maid Scotland fone brokyn apon eace,
For Cumyns ded and lofs off gud Wallace.
Yai led hym furth in feyr amang yaim aw,   1065
Kerle he myft, and yan ye Sothroune faw
Yan wyft he weill yat he betrayfyt was,
Towart ye fouth with hym quhen yai can pafs;
Zeit yai hym faid, in trewth he fuld nocht de,
King Edwarde wald kep hym in gud faufte,   1070
For hys honour in wer at he had wrocht.
Ye fayr bandys fo ftro blyt all hys thocht,
Credence yarto forfuth he coud not geyff,
He wyft full weill yai wald nocht let hym leyff.
A fals foull caufs ye Menteth for hym tauld,   1075
Quhen on yis wyfs gud Wallace he had fauld;
Sum off yaim faid, it was to faiff yair Lord,
Yai leid all out yat maid yat fals racord.
At ye Fawkyrk ye gud Stewart was flayn,
Our Cornielis raherfs yat in playn,   1080
On Madelan-day, yat auchtand zer befor,
Cumyns ded yar off it wytnefs mor,
At Robraftoun Wallace was trefonabilly
Yus falfly flewyn in hys gud chewalry,
In Glafkow ar wyft nocht off yis thing;   1085
Yus he was loft in bydyng off hys King.
South yai hym led by hakland ye weft land,
Delyuyrit hym in haift our Stilway fand.
Ye lord Clifurd and Wallang uk hym yar,
To Carleyll toun full faft with hym yai far,   1090

In prefoune hym ftad, yat was a gret dolour,
Yat houfs eftyr was callyt Wallace tour.
Sum men fen fyn faid, yat knew nocht weill ye cafs,
In Berweik yai to ded put gud Wallace.
Contrar is knawin fyrft be yis opinioun,   1095
For Scottfmen yan had haly Berweik toun,
And Scotland fre, quhill yat Soullis it gaiff
For Lord Cumyn till Ingland with ye laiff.
Ane oyir poynt is, ye traytours durft nocht pafs,
At fauld hym fa, quhar Scottfmen maifters wafs. 1100
Ye thrid poynt is, ye commownys off Ingland,
Quhat yai defyr, yai will nocht undirftand,
Yat thing be don, for wytnes at may be.
Na credence gyff forthyr yan yai may fe
To fe hym de Edwarde had mar defyr,   1105
Yan to be Lord off all ye gret Empyr.
For yis caufe yai kepyt hym fa lang,
Quhill ye commouns mycht on to London gang.
Allace, Scotland, to quhom fall yow compleyn!
Allace, fra payn quha fall yow now refreyn !   1110
Allace, yi help is falfslie brocht to ground,
Yi Chyftane in braith bandys is bound!
Allace, yow has now loft yi Gyd off lycht !
Allace, quha fall defend ye in yi rycht !
Allace, yi payn approchis wondyr ner,   1115
With forow fone yow mon be fet on feyr!
Yi Gracioufs God, yi grettaft Gouernour,
Allace, our neir is cummyn hys fatell hour !
Allace, quha fall ye beit now off yi baill !
Allace, quhen fall off harmes yow be haill !   1120
                                         Quha

Quh i fall ye defend! quha fall ye now mak fre!
Allace, in wer quha fall yi helpar be!
Quha fall ye help! quha fall ye now radem!
Allace, quha fall ye Saxons fra ze flem!
I can no mar, bot befek God off Grace,   1125
Ye to reftor in haift to rychtwyfnace:
Sen gud Wallace may fuccour ye no mar,
Ye lofs off hym encreffyt mekill cayr.
Now off hys men in Glafkow ftill at lay,
Quhat forow raifs quhen yai hym myft away.   1130
Ye cruell payn, ye wofull compleynyng,
Yaroff to tell it war our hewy thing;
I will lat be, and fpek off it na mar,
Litill rahers is our mekill off cayr,
And pryncipally quhar redemptioun is nayn,   1135
It helpis nocht to tell yar petoufs mayn;
Ye deid yaroff is ftill in remembrance,
I will lak flaik off forow ye ballance.
Bot Longaweill to Lowchmabar couth pafs,
And yar he hecht, quhar gud Prynce Edwarde was,
Out off Scotland he fuld pafs neuir mor,
Lofs off Wallace focht till hys hart fo for.
Ye realm off France he wowit he fuld neuir fe,
Bot wenge Wallace or yarfor ellis to de.
Yar he remaynd quhill cummyn off ye King,   1145
With Bruce in wer yis gud Knycht furth can ryng;
Remembrance fyn was in ye Bruce's buk,
Secund he was quhen yai Santt Jhonftoun tuk,
Folowed ye King at wynnyng off ye toun,
Ye Bruce yarfor gaiff hym full gret gardoun   1150

All

All Chartrys land ye gud King till hym gaiff,
Chartrys fen fyne off hys kyn is ye laiff.
Quharto fuld I in yat ftory wend,
Bot off my buk to mak a fynaill end ?
Robert ye Bruce com hame on ye ferd day   1155
In Scotland, eftyr Wallace was had away,
Till Lowchmaban, quhar yat he fand Edwart,
Quharoff he was gretly reioffyt in hart ;
Bot fra he wyft Wallace away was led,
So mekill bayll within hys breyft yar bred,   1160
Ner out off wyt he werthit for to weid.
Edwarde full fone yan till hys broyir zeid.
A fodane chance yis was in wo fra weill,
Gud Edwarde faid, yis helpis nocht a deill,
Lat murnyng be, it may mak na rameid,   1165
Ze haiff hym tynt, ze fuld rawenge hys deid ;
Bot for your caufs he tuk ye war on hand,
In your defens, and thryfs has fred Scotland,
Ye quhilk was tynt fra us and all our kyn,
War nocht Wallace, we neuir had entryt in.   1170
Merour he was off lauta and manheid,
In wer ye beft yat euyr power fall leid.
Had he likyt for till haiff tane zour croun,
Wald nane hym let yat was in yis regioun.
Had nocht beyne he, ze fuld had na entrefs   1175
Into yis realm, for trefoun and falfnes
Yat fall ye fe ; ye traytour yat hym fauld,
Fra zow he thinkis Dimbertane for till hauld ;
Sum comfort tak, and lat flaik off yis forow.
Ye King chargyt Edwarde apon ye morow,   1180

Radrefs

Radrefs to tak off wrang yat wrocht hym was,
Till Dawfwintoun he ordand hym to pafs,
And men off armys, gyff yai fand Cumyn yar,
Put hym to ded, for na deid yai fuld fpar.
Yai fand hym nocht. Ye King hymfelff hym flew 1185
Intill Dumfrefs, quhar witnes was inew.
Yat hapnys wrang our gret haift in a King,
Till wyrk be law it may fcaith mekill thing.
Me neds heroff na furthyr for to fchaw,
Quhow yat was done it was knawin to zow aw. 1190
Bot zong Douglace fyrft to ye King can pas,
In all hys wer bath wycht and worthy was;
Nor how ye King has tane on hym ye croun,
Off all yat her I mak bot fchort mentioun;
Nor how Lord Soullis gaiff Berweik toun away, 1195
How eftyr fyn fone tynt was Galloway;
How Jhon off Lorn agayn hys rycht King raifs,
On ayir fyd how Bruce had mony fais;
How bauld Breichin contrar hys King coud ryd,
Rycht few was yan in wer with hym to byd; 1200
Nor how ye north was gyffyn fra ye gud King,
Quhilk maid hym lang in paynfull wer to ryng.
Ay trew till hym was Jamys ye gud Douglace,
For Bruce rycht baid weill in mony place,
Undyr ye King he was ye beft Chyftayne, 1205
Bot Wallace raifs as Chyftane hym allane,
Yarfor till hym is no comparifoun,
As off a man, fauff reuerence off ye croun.
Bot fa mony off Douglace has beyn
Gud off a kyn, was neuir in Scotland feyn. 1210

Comperifoun

Comperifoun yat can I nocht weill declar,
Off Bruce buk as now I fpek no mar,
Maifter Barbour quhilk was a werthi clerk,
He faid ye Bruce amang hys oyir werk.
In yis mater prolixit I am almaift,   1215
To my purpofs breiflly I will me haift,
How gud Wallace was fet amang hys fayis,
To Londen with hym Clyffurd and Wallang gais,
Quhar King Edwarde was rycht fayn off yat fang,
Yai hym ftad intill a prefoune ftrang.   1220
Off Wallace end myfelff wald leiff for dreds,
To fay ve werft, bot rychtwyfnes me leds.
We tyrd hys lyff aw fwa werray trew,
Hys intell hour I will nocht fenzie now.
Menteth was fals, and yat was our weill knawin, 1225
Feill off yat kyn in Scotland yan was fawyn,
Chargyt to byd undyr ye gret jugement,
At King Robert aftyt in hys pa lement.
Yaroff I mak na langar contenuans,
Bot Wallace end in warld was difplefans ;   1230
Yarfor I cefs, and putts it nocht in rym.
Scotland may thank ye blyffyt happy tym
At he was born be prynfuall poynts twa,
Yis is ye fyrft, or yat we foryir ga.
Scotland he fred, and brocht it off thrillage,   1235
And now in Hewyn he has hys heretage.
As it prowyt be gud experians,
Wyfs clerkyfs zeit it kepeys in remembrans,
How yat a Monk off Bery Abbay yan,
Into yat tym a rycht religioufs man ;   1240

A

A zong Monk als with hym in ordour ftud,
Quhilk knew hys lyff was clene, perfyt and gud.
Yis fadyr Monk was wefyd with feknace,
Out off ye warld as he fuld pafs on cace.
Hys brodyr faw ye fpreit likly to pafs,   1245
A band off hym rycht ernyftly he coud afs,
To cum agayn, and fchaw hym off ye meid,
At he fald haiff at God for hys gud deid.
He grantyt hym, at hys prayer to preiff,
To cum agayn, gyff God wald geiff hym leiff.   1250
Ye fpreit changyt out off yis warldly payn,
In yat famyn hour cum to ye Monk agayn.
Sic th.ng has beyn, and is be woice and fycht,
Quhar he apperyt, yar fchawit fa mekill lycht;
Lyk till Lawntrins at illumynyt fo cler,   1255
At warldly lycht yarto mycht be na peyr.
A woice faid yus, God has me grantyt Grace
Yat I fall kep my promefs in yis place
Ye Monk was blyth off yis cler fygour fayr,
Bot a fyr-brand in hys for-heid he bayr,   1260
As yat hym thocht myfflikit all ye laive.
Quhar art yow, fpreit? anfuer, fa God me faive,
In purgatory. How lang fall ze be yair?
Bot halff ane hour to com and litill mair.
Purgatory is, I do yow weill to wytt,   1265
In ony place quhar God will it admitt.
Ane hour off fpace I was demed yar to be,
And yat paffis, fuppofs I fpek with ye.
Quhy has zow yat and all ye laiff fa ha'ill,
For off fcience I thocht me maift awaill?   1270

Quha

Quha prydis yarin, yat laubour is in waist,
For science cummys bot off ye Haly Gaift;
Eftir yin hour, quhar is yi paffage ewyn?
Quhen tym cummys, he faid, to leftand Hewyn.
Qunat tym is yat, I pray ze now declar.   1275
Twa ar on lyff mon be befor me yar.
Qunilk twa ar yai? Ye werete yow may ken.
Ye fyrft has beyn a gret flaar off men.
Now yai hym kep to martyr in Londoun toun
On Wednyffday, befor King and commoun;   1280
Is nayn on lyff at has fa mony flayn:
Brodyr, he faid, yat taill is bot in wayn,
For flauchtyr is to God abominabill.
Yan faid ye fpreit, forfuth yis is no fabill,
He is Wallace, Defendour off Scotland,   1285
For rychtwyfs wer yat he tuk apon land.
Yar rychtwyfnes is lowit our ye laive,
Yarfor in Hewyn he fall yat honour haive.
Syne a pure preyft is mekill to commend,
He tuk in thank quhat thing yat God hym fend, 1290
For dayly mefs, and heryng confeffioun,
Hewyn he fall haiff to leftand weryfoun.
I am ye thrid grantyt throw Godds Grace.
Brodyr, he faid, tell I yis in our place,
Yai will but deym, I oyir dreym or raive.   1295
Yan faid ye fpreit, yis witnyfs yow fall haive,
Zour bellys fall ryng, for ocht at ze do may,
Quhen yai hym fla, halff an hour off yat day.
And fo yai did, ye Monk wyft quhat yaim alyt,
Throuch braid Bretane ye woice yaroff was fcalyt. 1300

Ye

Ye fpreit tuk leyff at Goddis will to be.
Off Wallace end to her it is pete ;
And I wald nocht put men in gret dolour,
Bot lychtly pafs atour hys fatell hour.
On Wednyfday ye fals Sothroune furth brocht, 1305
Till martyr hym as yai befor had wrocht.
Rycht futh it is, a martyr Wallace was,
Als Offwald, Edmunt, Edward, and Thomas;
Off men in armes led hym a full gret rout.
With a bauld fpreit gud Wallace blent about,   1310
A preyft he afkyt, for God yat deit on tre.
King Edwarde yan cummandyt hys clerge,
And faid, I charge, on payn off lofs off lyff,
Nane be fa bald zon tyrand for to fchryff ;
He has rong lang in contrar my hienace.   1315
A blyft Byfchop fone prefent in yat place,
Off Canterbery he yan was rychtwyfs Lord,
Agayn ye King he maid yis rycht record,
And, myfelff fall her hys confeffioun,
Gyff I haiff mycht in contrar off yi croun ;   1320
And yow throw force will ftop me off yis thing,
I wow to God, quhilk is my rychtwyfs King,
Yat all Ingland I fall entyrdyt,
And mak it knawn zow ar ane herretyk.
Ye facrement off kyrk I fall hym geyff,   1325
Syn tak yi chos, to fterwe or lat hym leyff.
It war mar weill, in worfchip off yi croun,
To kep fic ane in lyk in yi bandoun,
Yan all ye land and gud at yow has refyd ;
Bot cowatyfs ye ay fra honour drefyd.   1330

Yow has lyff rongyn in wrangis deid,
Yat fall be feyn on ye or on yi feid.
Ye King gart charge yai fuld ye Byfchop ta,
Bot fad Lordys confellyt to lat hym ga.
All Inglifmen faid, yat hys defyr was rycht;   1335
To Wallace yan he rakyt in yair fycht,
And fadly herd hys confellioun till ane end.
Humbly to God hys fpreit he yar commend,
Lawly hym ferwyt with harty deuotioun
Apon hys kneis, and faid ane oryfoun.   1340
Hys leyff he tuk, and to Weft Monaftyr raid.
Ye lokmen yan yai bur Wallace but baid
On till a place hys martyrdome to tak,
For till hys ded he wald na forthyr mak.
Fra ye fyrft nycht he was tane in Scotland,   1345
Yai kepyt hym intill yat famyn band.
Na thing he had at fuld haiff doyn hym gud,
Bot Inglifmen hym feruit off carnaill fud.
Hys warldly lyff defyrd ye fuftenance,
Yocht he it gat in contrar off plefance.   1350
Yai threty dayis hys band yai durft nocht flaik,
Quhill he was boundyn on a fkamyll off ayk,
With yrn chenzeis yat was bath ftark and keyn.
A clerk yai fet to her quhat he wald meyn.
Zow Scott, he faid, yat gret wrang has don,   1355
Yi fatell hour, zow feis, approchis fon,
Yow fuld in mynd remembyr yi myfdeid,
At clerkis may, quhen yai yair pfalmis reid
For Cryftin faullis, yat makis yaim to pray,
In yair nowmyr yow may be ane off yai;   1360

      In

For now yow feis on fors yow mon decefs.

Yan Wallace faid, for all yi roid raherfs,

Yow has na charge, fuppofs at I did myfs,

Zon blyft Byfchop has hecht I fall haiff blyfs;

And trew I weill, yat God fall it admyt, 1365

Yi febyll words fall nocht my confcience fmit.

Comfort I haiff off way yat I fuld gang,

Maift payn I byd her our lang.

Yan faid yis clerk, our King offt fend ye till,

Yow mycht haiff had all Scotland at yi will, 1370

To hald off hym, and ceffyt off yi ftryff,

So as a Lord rongyn furth all yi lyff.

Yan Wallace faid, yow fpekis off mychty thing,

Had I leftyt, and gottyn my rychtwyfs King, 1375

Fra worthi Bruce had refawit hys croun,

I thocht haiff maid Ingland hys bandoun;

So uttraly it fuld beyn at hys will,

Quhat pleffyt hym, to fauff yi King or fpill.

Weill, faid yis clerk, yan zow rapents nocht,

Off wykkydnefs yow has a felloune thocht; 1380

Is nayn in warld yat has fa many flane,

Yarfor till afk, me think yow fuld be bane,

Grace off our King, and fyn at hys barnage.

Yan Wallace fmyld a litill at hys langage.

I grant, he faid, part Inglifmen I flew 1385

In my quarrel, me thocht nocht halff-enew.

I mowyt na wer bot to wyn our awin,

To God and man ye rycht full weill is knawin.

Yi fruftyr words dois nocht bot taris me,

I ye cummaund on Godds halff lat me be. 1390

A Schyrreff gart yis clerks fone fra hym pafs,
Rycht as yai durft yai grant quhat he wald afs.
A Pfaltyr buk Wallace had on hym euir,
Fra hys child-heid fra it wald nocht diffcuyr;
Bettyr he trowit in wiage for to fpeid,   1395
Bot yan he was difpulzeid off hys weid.
Yis grace he aft at Lord Clyffurd yat Knycht,
To lat hym haiff hys Pfaltyr buk in fycht;
He gert a preyft it oppyn befor hym hauld,
Quhill yai till hym had done all at yai wauld. 1400
Stedfaft he red, for ocht yai did hym yar,
Feill Sothroune faid, at Wallace feld na fayr.
Gud deuotioun fa was hys begynnyng,
Conteynd yarwith, and fair was hys endyng,
Quhill fpech and fpreit all at once can fayr 1405
To leftand Blyfs, we trow for euirmar.
I will nocht tell how he dewydyt was
In fyffe parts, and ordand for to pafs,
Bot yus hys fpreit be liklynes was weill.
Off Wallace lyff quha has a forthyr feill, 1410
May fchaw furth mar with witt and eloquence,
For I to yis haiff don my diligence.
Eftyr ye pruff got fra ye Latyn buk,
Quhilk Maiftyr Blayr in hys tym undyrtuk,
In fayr Latyn compild it till ane end,   1415
With yir witnes ye mar is to commend.
Byfchop Synclar yan Lord was off Dunkell,
He gat yis buk and confirmd it hymfell
For werray trew, yaroff he had na dreid,
Hymfelff had feyn gret **part** off Wallace deid. 1420

         Hys

Hys purpofs was for till haive fend it to Rom,
Our Fadyr off Kyrk yaron to gyff hys dom.
Bot Maiftyr Blayr, and als Schyr Thomas Gray,
Eftir Wallace yai leftyt mony day.
Yir twa knew beft off gud Schyr Wilzhams deid,
Fra faxteyn zer quhill nyne and twenty zeid.
Fortye and fyffe off age Wallace was cauld,
Yat tym yat he was to Sothroune fauld.
Yocht yis mater be nocht to all plefance,
Hys futhfaft deid was worthi till awance.   1430
All worthy men yat redys yis rurall dyt,
Blaym nocht ye buk fet I be unperfyt.
I fuld haive thank, fen I nocht trawaill fpard,
For my labour na man hecht me reward;
Na charge I had off King or oyir Lord,   1435
Gret harm I thocht hys gud deid fuld be fmord.
I haiff faid her ner as ye procefs gais,
And fenzied nocht for freindfchip nor for fais.
Cofts hereoff was no man bond to me,
In yis fentence I had na will to be;   1440
Bot in als mekill as I raherfyt nocht
Sa worthely as nobill Wallace wrocht.
Bot in a poynt, I grant, I faid amyfs,
Yir twa Knychts fuld be blam-t for yis,
Ye Knycht Wallace off Cragge rychtwyfs Lord, 1445
And Liddaill als gert me mak wrang record.
On Allyrtoun-mur ye croun he tuk a day.
To get battaill as my autor will fay,
Yir twa gart me fay yat ane oyir wyfs,
Till Maiftyr Blayr we did fum part off dyfpefs, 1450

Go

Go nobill buk, fullfillyt off gud fentens,

Suppofs yow be baran off eloquence.

Go worthi buk, fullfillyt off futhfaft deid,

Bot in langage off help yow has gret neid.

Quhen gud makars rang weill into Scotland,   1455

Gret harm was it yat nane off yaim ze fand ;

Zeit yar is part yat can ze weill awance,

Now byd yi tym, and be a remembrance.

I yow befek, off your beneuolence,

Quha will nocht low, lak nocht my eloquence.   1460

It is weill knawin I am a rural man,

For her is faid as gudly as I can.

My fpreit felys na termys afpriance,

Now befek God, yat Gyffar is off Grace,

Maid hell and erd, and fet ye hewyn abuff,   1465

Yat he us grant off hys der leftand luff.

* A few words torn away here in the M. S.

F I N I S.

VERSES not in the manufcript, or not in the copy
tranfmitted to the Publifhers, but which appear in
the former printed Editions, and which are indeed
for moft part neceffary for completing the fenfe of
the paffages with which they are connected.

B O O K I.——Verse, 383.

Sanct Martine's fifh, faid, Scot, we would have.
Wallace meekly, &c.

B O O K II.——V. 165.

The flower of youth into his tender age,
By fortune, &c.

B O O K IV.——V. 642.

Then Wallace faid, we labour all in vain ;
To flay commons it helpeth us right nought,
But their Chiftains, that hath them hither brought,
Might we work fo that one of them were flain,
So fore offay, &c.

B O O K VI.——V. 63.

Defiring ay his manhood to prove
In courage, &c.

V. 78.

That never in warld out of his mind was brought.
Now leave thy mirth, &c.

V. 158.

The worthy Scots which cruel were and keen,
Among the Southerone, &c.

V. 835.

Wallace purpofed that place for to affail.
A woman told, when the Captain was gone,
Good men of fence into that place were none.
They filled the dyke with earth and timber haill,
Undid the gate, &c.

BOOK VIII.——V. 961.

Of Saint Johnftoun now I have remembrance,
There I have been, &c.

BOOK VIII.——V. 660.

Though he refufed it laftingly to bear.
The people all, &c.

V. 1518.

Richt at his will they have confented haill,
For no kin thing, &c.

BOOK IX.——V. 177.

Unto Rochel I would ye gart them fail,
For Inglifhmen, &c.

V. 579.

Entered he was into Bothwel again,
Sir John Sewart that came, &c.

V. 901.

That all the lave of us abafed be,
Then fray the firft, &c.

Good

B O O K X.——V. 795.

Good Keirly paft, had been with Wallace long,
And done full well in many fellon throng.
This Keirly then that could with Wallace fare,
Will. Ker he hight, mine author can declare.
Keirly in Irifh, is but Ker Little call'd,
In Carrick he had heritage of ald.
His forbear, which ay worthy was of hand,
Saint David King him brought out of Ireland;
Syne at Dummnoir, where firft Norways came in,
This Ker made great difcomfiture of their kin,
With feven hundred vanquifhed nine thoufand,
Some drown'd in Doun, fome flain upon the land.
Thofe whole lands the good King gave him until,
How Wallace paft now further fpeak I will.
Among merchants, &c.

B O O K XI.——V. 469.

But we thee had, we fhall gar thy fides fow.
Of this I afk, &c.

N. B. **Add to** the Argument of the Ninth Book.

—Takes Perth—Battle of Black Ironfide, 1298—
Wallace **takes Lochlevin—And Airth—Bu**rns the
Englifh at Dunbarton—**Takes** Rofneith—Sir Willi-
am Douglas takes Sanquhar—Wallace takes many
Places—Siege of Dundee—Wallace's **Perfon.**

MANUSCRIPT COPY

H E N R Y's P O E M.

THE only manuscript known of Henry's History of Wallace, and from which undoubtedly all the printed copies have been taken, however much in point of orthography they have deviated from it, is now in the Advocates' Library at Edinburgh.

It was written by John Ramsay, who subscribes it in the following words:

" Explicit Vita Nobilissimi Defensoris Scotiæ, videlicet, Willielmi Wallace Militis, per me Johannem Ramsay, Anno Domini Millesimo Quadringentesimo Octuagesimo Octavo." Some words which he had added are tore away.

" The Life ends of the most Noble Defender of Scotland, viz. of William Wallace, Knight. By me John Ramsay, in the year of our Lord, 1488."

This is not written in the ordinary form of a notorial attestation. The writer probably had some other professional character than that of a Notary Public.

He seems to have proceeded in his work in a devotional manner, for the following prayer, in Monkish Latin, is also inserted,

" Jesu, Salvator! ex Jussu mihi exponere, ad finem dignum, prædictum Librum, atque benig-num."

" Grant

" Grant to me to difplay the forefaid book, and to bring it an honourable and gracious conclufion."

This may have been Henry's prayer; but appears rather to have been compofed by Ramfay, and to have been ufed by him as often as one of the Books of the Poem was ended, and another was to begin.

It is impoffible to know what liberties he may have taken with the original work. It is to be prefumed they were not very great. Henry had completed his Hiftory of Wallace in the time of Major's infancy, viz. about the year 1446, and probably copies of it were now in the hands of many perfons.

The orthography of the manufcript may be reckoned to be fuch as was common in Ramfay's time. He may alfo be fuppofed to have taken the liberty of dividing the Poem into Books in a manner fuitable to his own fancy or conveniency. In his manufcript, the Poem confifts of eleven Books: But the divifion might be altered for the better, as in fome parts the narration is improperly broken, and the Books bear not a fit proportion in length to one another.

The Sections of the Books into Chapters, which have hitherto appeared in the printed copies, are not to be found in the manufcript. But fuch Sections in Henry's Poem, in which fo many events are related, would tend to the relief and direction of the reader.

It is a pity that the additional words to Ramfay's fubfcription have been torn away. It may be fuppofed to have been occafioned by the injurious effect of

time,

time. Perhaps he had made fome mention of **Henry.** Or perhaps he had written **more** fully concerning him-felf.

It may be reckoned **no** improbable conjecture, that he was **one of thofe who wrote Chronicles in the Mo-** nafteries.

From writs extant at Perth, which belonged **to the** Carthufian **Monaftery there, it** appears **that " a reli-** gious **man,** Dean **John** Ramfay, **of the** Houfe of the **Valley of** Virtue, **of the** Carthufian Order, near the **Burgh** of Perth," was Procurator for the faid Monaf-**tery, May** 23, 1493.

The Procuratorfhip was an ufual ftep to the dignity **of** Prior. Before 1498, John Ramfay ceafes **to be** mentioned **as** Procurator. But in April, that year John, whofe firname is not mentioned in any of the **writs** at Perth, is prior, and continues in the Prior's **office till his death in** 1501. **He was probably the** ame perfon who had been **Procurator.**

The tranfcriber of Henry's Book was therefore, **perhaps, a Charter**houfe Monk, who near the end of **his Life,** rofe to be Prior of the Convent.

In the earlier part of his Life, it is not impoffible he **might have been** well acquainted with Henry, and had **heard him** often recite his **hiftories. He might alfo have** been the writer of the " Liber Carthufianorum **de Perth," which was written in the Monaft**ery there, **and which is faid to contain, with fome** additions, **a** Compend in twelve Books **of what** Fordun and Bow-maker had **written.**

No

No fufpicion however needs **to arife** of his having wifhed to be confidered as the **Author of the** Hiftory **of** Wallace.

A poor blind man, as Henry was, who, if really **in** any degree connected with a Religious Order, was unfit **by** reafon of his blindnefs for performing many **of the offices of it,** and who wandered through the country expecting as a mendicant his food and rayment, might **fay** concerning himfelf, that " he would leave it to learned clerks to treat of **the** fubtile parts of theology," that " he was not eloquent," and that " **it was well known, he was a rural or** fimple **man."**

But the **accurate writer of the** manufcript, efpecially if he was a Carthufian Monk, would not have **fpo**ken of himfelf in terms fo humiliating.

N O T E,

Since **the** above was written, Mr Pinkerton has **fa**voured **the** Public with his valuable Edition of Barbour's **Hiftorical** Poem of the Acts of King Robert Bruce. He has caufed **it to be** printed according to **the** orthography **of a** manufcript copy in the Advocates' Library.

I find that John Ramfay was alfo the **writer of this** manufcript; and that **he** wrote it in **1489,** which was **the year after he** had finifhed his copy **of Henry's Poem.**

The words of the fubfcription undoubtedly are,

" Finitur

" Finitur Codicillus de Virtutibus & Actibus Belli-cofis, viz. Domini Roberti Broys, quondam Scottorum Regis illuftriffimi, raptim fcriptus per me Johannem Ramfay, ex Juffu venerabilis & circumfpecti viri, viz. Magiftri Symonis Lochmalony de Ouchtermuinfye Vicarii bene digni. Anno Domini Millefimo Quadringentefimo Octuagefimo nono."

" The Book is ended of the virtues and warlike Acts, viz. of Lord Robert Bruce, formerly the illuftrious King of Scots ; haftily written by me John Ramfay, at the command of a venerable and circumfpect man, viz. Mafter Simon Lochmalony, the worthy Vicar of Ouchtermuinfye. In the year of our Lord, 1489."

The lands of Lochmalony, in the Parifh of Kilmeny, in the north eaft part of Fife, gave a furname to a family in Fife which fubfifted for a confiderable time.

June 27, 1466. Allan Lochmalony of that Ilk, was one of thofe gentlemen who fettled the marches of fome lands belonging to the Monaftery of Dunfermling. Sir Robt. Sibbald's Hift. of Fife, p. 89.

March 31, 1517. Alexander Lochmalonie of that Ilk, was one of thofe perfons who were appointed by the Sheriffs, to affix valuations to the lands in the County of Fife. Ibid. p. 82, 83.

Simon Lochmalony, Vicar of Moonfie, the venerable friend of Ramfay, muft have been a defcendant of this family.

The

The gaelic word " Ochter," or " Auchter," which fignifies the Brae or high Ground. is prefixed to the names of many places on the north fide of Forth.

The Parifh Church of Moonfie, about two miles north weft from Cupar in Fife, is fituated on the top of a hill. In a record, March 11, 1·17, it has the name of Auchter Monfey. Ibid. p. 86.

William Malvoifin Bifhop of St Andrews, who died in 1733, gave this Church to the Monaftery of Scotland well. The words in his Charter of Donation are " Ecclefiam Sanctæ Trinitatis de Urhithumenefyn, hoc eft, Moonfey." Ibid. p. 111.

In confequence of this gift, the Friars of the monaf-tery enjoyed the Rectory tithes, and employed a Vi-çar to officiate in the Parifh.

An apology might be reckoned neceffary to Mr Pinkerton. But as he refides in England, and thereby has not the opportunity of eafily acquiring information concerning fuch minute particulars, he will not be difpleafed to fee this illuftration of Ramfay's fubfcription.

CHRONOLOGY

OF

Sir WILLIAM WALLACE.

WALLACE was about fixteen years of age when he was put to the fchool at Dundee. He was twenty nine years of age when he fuffered death at London, Auguft, 1305.

Some affirmed that he was forty five years of age, when he was fold to the Englifh, in 1305. But Henry fays, however much they might be difpleafed, he muft affert that the contrary was the truth.

1292.

Sir Malcolm Wallace of Ellerflie, near Paifley in the fhire of Renfrew, finding himfelf oppreffed by the Englifh, who were then affuming a fuperiority over the country, flies from his own houfe of Ellerflie, with his eldeft fon Malcolm, to the Lennoz, viz. to Dunbarton-fhire.

His lady, Margaret Crawfurd, who was daughter of Hugh Crawfurd of Loudoun in the fhire of Air, is fent for protection by her father to his aged uncle, of the name of Crawfurd, who was Laird of Kilfpindy in the Braes of the Carfe of Gowrie in Perth-fhire. She takes with her her fon William, who was not then fully fixteen years of age.

William is put to the fchool at Dundee.

According

1295.

According to Henry, fo early as this year, an Eng-
lishman **of** the name of Selby, had by fome **means or**
other, been appointed to the office of Conftable, Cap-
tain or Governor, of the Port and Caftle of Dundee.
This Port being thereby acceffible to the Englifh, they
were crowding into the interior part of the Kingdom.

William Wallace, who had been taken from fchool,
and had **refided fome** time with his mother and great
uncle at Kilfpindy, is fent on **a** meffage to Dundee.
The Conftable's fon infults **him,** and is flain by him.

A Juftice Air is appointed to be held **at** Dundee.
Wallace and his mother flie from Kilfpindy firft, to
Dunipace in Stirling-fhire, the parfon of which was **a**
brother of Wallace's father. Afterwards **to Ellerflie.**

Wallace is now fully eighteen years of age.

Before this time, Sir Malcolm Wallace and his el-
deft fon had been killed in a fkirmifh on Loudoun-hill.
Hugh Crawfurd of Loudoun alfo was now dead. His
fon, Sir Reginald, according to the hereditary right
in the family, was acting **as** Sheriff of Air. Henry
Peircy was Governor **of the** Caftle of Air.

February, March, 1296.

Wallace refides **for fome time** with **his** uncle Sir
Reginald Crawfurd, at **Corfbie,** in the fhire of Air.
Afterwards refides at Richardtoun in the fame fhire,
with **Sir** Richard Wallace of Richardtoun, his father's
elder brother.

April 23, 1296.

Wallace, who had gone **to** fifh in the **water** of Irvine,

vine, kills fome Englifhmen. He leaves the houfe of Sir Richard his uncle, accompanied only by a page.

April, May, **June,** July, 1296.

Goes to Auchincraif in Air-fhire, where his coufin, a gentleman of the name of Wallace dwelt. This gentleman's houfe was not far from Air, and in the neighbourhood of Laglane-wood.

In one of his excurfions to the town of Air, he kills a Churl, or ftrong Englifhman. In another he kills Peircie's fteward, and, being taken, is imprifoned in the Caftle of Air.

Falls fick in the prifon. Being thought dead, is thrown out of the Caftle. His nurfe takes him up, and conceals him in her own houfe till his recovery.

July, 1296.

Returns to his uncle's houfe at Richardtoun. Is there joined by fome friends. His party amounts to fifty in number. They defeat fome Englifh on Loudoun-hill, and remain in Clyde's-wood twenty days.

(N. B. It is to be remarked, that during the courfe of this year, war had been carried on with the Englifh in other parts of the Kingdom. March 3c, 1296, happened the fiege of Berwick. April 5, John Baliol renounced in a formal manner the allegiance which he had fworn to Edward. April 28, happened the fiege of Dunbar. July 2, Baliol refigned the Kingdom wholly into the hands of Edward. The Scotifh Barons were obliged to come immediately in great numbers, to profefs their fubmiffion to Edward.

Still

Still however the party in the weft, headed by Wallace, were difturbing the Englifh in the conqueft they had made.)

Auguft, 1296.

Wallace is perfuaded by his uncle, Sir Reginald Crawfurd, to make a truce with Peircy for ten months. His companions then difperfe, and he goes to refide with his uncle at Corfbie.

In a few days he goes with fifteen men to the town of Air. Kills an Englifh Buckler Player, who had defied him. Retreats with his men to Laglane wood. Returns to Corfbie, where he continues fixteen days.

September, 1296.

Engages in a bloody adventure in his way to Glafgow. Flies to Lennox Hall in Dunbartonfhire, the feat of Malcolm Earl of Lennox, where he is joined by fixty men.

They take their rout northwards. Spoil the caftle cf Gargunnock in Stirling-fhire. Reft one night in the foreft of Kincardine. Come to Methven wood in the neighbourhood of Perth. Wallace, with feven of his men, enter Perth, where they remain unknown fome days.

(N. B. Henry in this part of his hiftory, viz. B. 4. v. 342, obferves that Wallace contended with the Englifh exactly fix years and feven months. That he obtained peace for Scotland. That when he left his country, probably meaning when he went to France, Scotland again was conquered.

October, 1296.

Wallace and his fixty men **defeat** ninety Englifh **near Kinclevin, in Perthfhire. They take** the caftle **of Kinclevin, and remain** in it feven days. They burn **the caftle, and** retire **to Shortwood fhaw,** where **a** bloody battle is fought.

The night after the battle, they go to Cargill wood. In **the morning they** return to the wood of Methven, where they remain two days.

November, 1296.

They are in Elcho park. Some days pafs in the ad-venture of Wallace's miftrefs in Perth. Battle along the north fide of the river Erne.

Wallace next morning in the houfe of **a** widow in the Carfe of Torwood. Next day at Dunipace. Three nights at Dundaff, the feat of Sir John Graham. One night **in** Bothwell **muir.**

December, 1296.

At Gillbank in the Parifh of Lefmahagow and fhire of Lanark, the feat of Auchinleck of that ilk. Is there joined by fome friends.

December, 1296.——March, 1297.

During **the** winter Wallace refides **at** Gillbank, fome-times goesto Lanark; where he marries the daughterand heirefs of the deceafed Hugh Braidfoot of Lamington.

Lochmaben caftle is taken. Some other exploits are mentioned.

April, **May, June,** 1297.

Wallace **dwells** with his wife in Lanark. She is kil-led by the **Englifh** after the birth **of** her daughter.

Many

Many exploits performed by him. **His fame is fpread abroad, and his party increafed.**

July, 1297.

The ten months truce expires. The patriots chufe Wallace to be their chief. He affembles forces in Clydefdale. Defeats Edward's army near **Biggar. Is made Warden, or** Governor of Scotland, **at the Foreft Church, or Selkirk.**

Auguft, &c. 1297.

Appoints fheriffs, and holds juftice courts. Reftores **the** patriots to the poffeffion of their lands. The whole country is fubject to him from Gamlifpath to Ur Water.

November, December, 1297. January, 1297—8.

Wallace refides at Black Craigs, in the parifh of New Cumnock and fhire of Air. His houfhold is there eftablifhed.

February, 1297—8.

Makes peace with the Englifh in the **church** of Ruthglen in the fhire of Lanark. Goes again to his caftle of Black Bog, or Black Craigs.

April, 1298.

Edward holds a council at Carlifle. A ftratagem is **there concerted for deftroying many** of the **Scots barons in Edward's** Barns **at Air.**

June 18, 1298.

Many **of** the Scots barons are treacheroufly put to **death in the Barns at Air.**

(**N. B.** This event is more fuitable to the ftate of the country in 1297. After the above date, there is no more **any confiftency in Henry's** chronology.)

K 2   REMARKABLE

REMARKABLE PERSONS

OF THE

SCOTISH PARTY.

AUCHINLECK.

NICOL de Auchinleck, Baron of Auchinleck, in the shire of Air, was compelled, along with many other Scotish barons, to swear fealty to Edward I, King of England, Auguft 5, 1296.

He was married to an aunt of Wallace, fifter of Sir Reginald Crawfurd of Loudoun.

Wallace, who had unfortunately loft moft of his men in his firft northern expedition, came to this gentleman, at his houfe of Gillbank, in the fhire of Lanark, December, 1296. Auchinleck entertained him kindly; and he, and his fon, who was then nineteen years of age, and many other gentlemen, declared they would join with Wallace in the defign of recovering the liberties of Scotland.

Wallace refided with him many months, and was particularly affifted by him in putting to death Hefilrig, the Englifh fheriff of Lanark, and in burning the Barns at Air.

This patriotic baron, of whom Henry gives a moft excellent character, was afterwards killed by fome of the Englifh at Air.

The

The family of Auchinleck of that ilk, continued till the reign of James **IV.** The heirefs **was then** marr ied to Sir William Douglas, **a** younger **fon of** the Earl of Angus, and anceftor **of the** Douglaffes of Glenbervie. But the King gave the **eftate of** Auchinleck, which by recognition had fallen into his hands, to Thomas Bof-well, anceftor of the Bofwells **of** Auchinleck.

BARCLAY.

Patrick and Walter de Barclays, fuppofed to be the anceftors of the Barclays of Crawfurd-John, and Kil-bierny, fwore fealty to Edward in 1296.

One of them was the patriotic friend **of** Wallace, **and** affifted more efpecially in burning the Barns at Air, in which were contained **many of** the Englifh. According to Henry, **he** had good reafon **to** join in this act of revenge, as, among others, fome **of** the Bar-clays had been cruelly put **to death in thefe** Barns or Barracks, June **18, 1298.**

BISSET.

William Biffet, anceftor of the Biffets of that ilk, **was one of the arbitrators** between the competitors for the Crown of Scotland, in 1291.

He is probably **the fame who** was the friend of Wal-lace. " The good Biffet," as Henry calls him, was well acquainted with the Counties of Perth and Fife, and could give ufeful direction to Wallace, when en-gaged in thefe Counties.

He

He took an active part in the second siege of the town of Perth. He fought in the battle at Black Iron-side in Fife, which according to Henry, happened a long time posterior to the date commonly assigned. But in that battle he was killed by Sir John Siward the English General, and the loyal Scots greatly lamented his death.

BLAIR.

Sir Bryce Blair, baron of Blair in Air-shire, was one of those to whom Wallace applied for aid, after his first northern expedition in 1296.

He was loyal to his country, and is not in the list of those who swore fealty to Edward. According to Henry, he was one of the Scotish barons who were put to death, by a cruel stratagem at Air, June 18, 1298.

He left no issue, it is said, but was succeeded by his brother David, ancestor of the Blairs of that ilk, in the County of Air.

BLAIR.

Mr John Blair, a younger son of Blair of that ilk, or of the family of Blair of Balthayock in Perth-shire, was a fellow student with Wallace in the school at Dundee, in 1292.

Being intended for the church, he went to Paris to finish his education, and there received Priest's Orders. He returned to Scotland before the end of the year 1296. Wallace, who was then at Gillbank, employed him in messages to Sir Bryce Blair and others, to engage them to join in refifting the ufurpations of the Englifh.

He became the conftant companion of Wallace, who put great confidence in him. He performed the prieft-ly offices ; and, like fome other clergymen of that time, was ambitious of being confidered as a brave warrior.

When he accompanied Wallace in his fecond voy-age to France, he acted with remarkable courage in the encounter with John of Lyn, an Englifh pirate.

He is faid to have become a Monk at Dunfermling after Wallace's death, and to have changed his name from John to Arnold, perhaps becaufe under the for-mer name he had been a fhedder of blood.

He and Mr Thomas Gray joined in writing a Latin Hiftory of Wallace, to which Henry often refers. But the Latin Chronicle, which bears the name of Arnold Blair's Relations, feems to be falfely afcribed to Mr John Blair.

BOYD.

Sir Robert de Boyd, anceftor of the Earls of Kil-marnock, and now alfo of the Earls of Errol, fwore fealty to Edward in 1296. He afterwards joined Wal-lace, and performed many acts of valour.

He died about the year 1300, while Wallace was continuing his exertions in the behalf of his country.

BRAIDFOOT.

Hugh Braidfoot of Lamington in the fhire of La-nark, died about the year 1295.

His

His wife also being dead, and Hesilrig, the English sheriff of Lanark. having killed his only son, an orphan daughter remained, who was heiress of her father's estate. She paid tribute to the English, that she might be allowed to live in peace in her own house at Lanark.

This lady, who obtained the honour of being the wife of Wallace, and of transmitting his blood to posterity, is particularly described by Henry. " She was humble, amiable, benign, wary, and wise ; courteous and sweet. Her mind was filled with noble sentiments. Her tongue was well governed. Her countenance was healthful. She purchased a good name, and kept herself free from blame with any man."

Hesilrig sought to marry her to his own son. But Wallace having seen her in his expeditions from Gillbank to Lanark, made to her proposals of marriage, which were accepted.

She bore to him a daughter. But shortly after the birth of her child, having deceived a party of English who were pursuing after her husband, they cruelly put her to death.

Wallace's daughter, heiress of Lamington, was married to a gentleman of the surname of Schaw, from whom, says Henry, many goodly men have descended.

Afterwards she, or a descendant of her's, who was also heiress of Lamington, was married to Sir William Baillie of Hoprig in East-Lothian, ancestor of the Baillies of Lamington.

Their

Their defcendant, Henrietta, likewife heirefs of the fame eftate, was married to Robert Dundas of Arnifton, Prefident of the College of Juftice.

Whofe daughter, Elizabeth, heirefs of Lamington, and lineal reprefentative of the daughter of Wallace, was married to a brave fea-officer, the late admiral, Sir John Lockhart Rofs, who was Member of Parliament for Lanark-fhire.

BYRD.

B. 7. v. 250. " Inftead of Cleland and Boyd," read " Cleland and Byrd." This reading is according to the former printed editions, and is the moft accurate.

B. 8. v. **233.** Henry fays, " Boyd, Barclay, Byrd, and Lawder, that were wight," or brave and powerful.

Byrd, whoever he was, is reprefented by Henry as a man of valour, and a friend of Wallace. He affifted in burning the Barns at Air, and afterwards in expelling the warlike bifhop of Durham, and others, out of Scotland.

It has been fuppofed that Byrd has been written for Bard. Fergus de Bard, and John and Robert Bards, anceftors of families of the furname of Baird, fwore fealty to Edward, in 1296.

In a charter by John Bell to John de Rollock, in, or about the year 137c, the feal of John Dubyrd, at the time one of the baillies of Perth, was appended.

There have been perfons in Scotland of the furname of Bird in latter times. But perhaps it may be inftructed,

ſtructed, by ſuch as have better opportunity, to be only according to the vulgar pronunciation of the ſurname of Bard.

CAMPBELL.

Sir Nichol or Neil Campbell of Lochow, anceſtor of
the Dukes of Argyle, ſwore fealty to Edward, July
29, 1296.

Henry calls him " the good Knight of Lochow,"
and ſays, he had been with Wallace at the ſchool of
Dundee.

He, and Duncan, uncle of John Macdougal of Lorn,
ſought Wallace's aſſiſtance againſt Macfadzan, an I-
riſhman, to whom Edward, with the approbation of
John of Lorn, had given their lands.

Macfadzan was in the intereſt of the Engliſh, and
led an army of Iriſh, who were barbarouſly waſting
the north-weſt part of Scotland. Wallace, with the
Campbells and Macdougals, defeated them, and ſlew
Macfadzan, who had fled with fifteen men into a cave
under Criagmore. A ſtone monument, with Macfadzan's head upon the top of it, was erected, in memo-
ry of the victory, upon the hill of Craigmore.

CHARTERIS.

Sir Thomas Charteris, commonly called Thomas of
Longueville, was a native of France, deſcended of an
ancient family in that country, and heir of their eſtates.

When at the Court of Philip le Bel, who ſucceeded
to the Crown of France in 1285, he had a diſpute with
a French

a French nobleman, and killed him in the King's preſence. He made his eſcape, and the King refuſed to grant him a pardon.

During the ſpace of ſixteen years, he infeſted the ſeas as a pirate, and was denominated " the Red Reaver," becauſe of the red flags which he diſplayed from his ſhips.

According to Henry's chronology, May 1301, or 1302, Wallace, in his way to France, encountered him, and took him priſoner. The French King, at Wallace's deſire, pardoned him, and beſtowed upon him the honour of Knighthood.

Sir Thomas, however, would not remain in France, but came with Wallace to Scotland, to whom he was ever after a faithful friend, and aided him in his exploits.

When Wallace was carried a priſoner into England, Sir Thomas Charteris retired to Lochmaben where he continued till Robert Bruce began to aſſert his right to the Crown of Scotland. He joined Bruce, and according to Henry, who refers to Barbour's Hiſtory of Bruce, was ſecond to that King, or the firſt who followed him into the water at the taking of Perth, January 8, 1312—13.

Bruce gave him lands in reward of his bravery.

Truth may be found mixed with fable in many of Henry's relations. There was a French Knight with Bruce, when Perth was taken, at the time abovementioned. The lands of Kinfauns in the neighbourhood of Perth, were long the property of a family
of

of the furname of Charteris, though a part of thefe lands fometimes changed its poffeffors. In the Caftle of Kinfauns is kept a two handed fword, which is faid to have belonged to Thomas of Longueville. Mr Henry Adamfon, in his Mufe's Threnodie, B. 6, fays,

"Kinfauns, which famous Longueville
Sometime did hold; whofe ancient fword of fteel
Remains unto this day, and of that land
Is chiefeft evident."

About thirty years ago, when the burying vault in the Parifh Church of Kinfauns happened to be open-ed, I was fhewed a helmet made of thick leather, or of fome fuch ftuff, painted over with broad ftripes of blue and white, which I was told, was part of the fic-titious armour in which the body of Thomas of Lon-gueville had been depofited. Henry fays, he was of large ftature, and the helmet indeed was a very large one.

Some perfons of the furname of Charteris, Lairds of Kinfauns, and of Cuthilgourdy, were provofts of Perth, and would make a diftinguifhed figure in the heroic annals of Perth, if the old writs of that city were pro-perly difplayed.

The eftate of Kinfauns afterwards belonged to a fa-mily of the furname of Blair, the heirefs of which was married to John Lord Gray, father of the prefent lord.

But long before the time affigned to Thomas of Longueville, there were families of the furname of Charteris in Scotland. Andrew de Charteris, who fwore fealty to Edward in 1296, is faid to have been anceftor of Charteris of Amisfield.

James

CLELAND.

James Cleland of that ilk, in the County of Lanark, anceſtor of the Clelands of that ilk, and of ſome other families of the ſame ſurname, was a near couſin of Wallace.

He joined Wallace in 1296, and was with him in many of his exploits, particularly in taking priſoner Thomas of Longueville, commonly called the Red Reaver.

CLIMACE.

While Wallace was the ſecond time in France, Edward, with a great **army,** entered Scotland. He met with little oppoſition, **and** got poſſeſſion of all the caſtles and towns as far as Rofs-ſhire. Many of the loyaliſts were taken priſoners and ſent to London. Others fled, chiefly to the ſhire of Rofs, and to the Iſles.

Sir John Ramſay of Auchterhouſe, **and Ruthven of that ilk,** fled to the houſe of their couſin the Lord of Fyllorth in Aberdeen-ſhire. He went with them immediately through the Murray Lands.

" So," fays Henry, " they found a gentle and worthy Knight **called Climace,** who always had been ſteady, and **maintained himſelf well** among his enemies. His purpoſe **ever** was to make no peace with Edward, and he had ſlain many of the invaders.

" **This Knight** led Ramſay, Ruthven, and others in Rofs-ſhire. They built a ſtrong caſtle at Stockfoord, which gave them the command of that country, and the opportunity of doing much hurt to the Engliſh."

Ruthven afterwards took refuge for fome time in Birnam wood.

After Wallace had returned from France, and was gathering a party near Perth, " the Knight Climes of Rofs, or from Rofs, and the barons who were with him, came into the Murray Lands with their good chevalry. The good Knight took the houfe of Nairn, and flew the Captain and Garrifon. From thence they paffed into Buchan."

William Earl of Rofs was at this time a prifoner in England. Climace was perhaps his fon or brother.

In the reign of Robert II, the lands and barony of Philorth, became the property of Sir Alexander Frazer, anceftor of the Lords of Salton, by his marriage with Johanna, fecond daughter and co-heirefs of the Earl of Rofs.

CRAWFURD.

Margaret Crawfurd, Lady Wallace of Ellerflie, daughter of Hugh Crawfurd of Loudoun, wife of Sir Malcolm, and mother of Sir William Wallace of Ellerflie.

" She was fair," Henry fays, " and of good fame and renown."

She feems to have been the fecond or laft wife of Sir Malcolm Wallace, and to have had no other child but William.

In 1292, fhe and her fon were fent by her father, to the protection of her father's uncle, the old Laird of Kilfpindy, in the Carfe of Gowrie, a diftrict of Perthfhire.

shire. While she was there her father died, and her husband and his eldest son Malcolm, were killed in a skirmish with the English

In 1295, after her son had killed young Selby at Dundee, she fled with him from Perth-shire. They made their escape in the dress of pilgrims, and pretended to be going to the shrine of St Margaret at Dunfermling, who was a Saint much regarded by the English.

She resided about three years at Ellerslie near Paisley, under the protection of her brother Sir Reginald. At last, he being dead, and her son's enemies giving her much trouble, she fled from that place, in 1298, and disguised as a pilgrim fought a sanctuary at Dunfermling. There in the month of December she sickened and died. Wallace could not go at that time to Dunfermling, but sent Jop his herald, and Mr John Blair as a clergyman to take care of her interment. They buried her at Dunfermling in a very costly and honourable manner.

CRAWFURD.

Hugh Crawfurd of Loudoun in the shire of Air, father of Lady Wallace of Ellerslie. Henry calls him Rannald or Reginald. Other authorities give him the name of Hugh.

CRAWFURD.

Sir Reginald Crawfurd of Loudoun, succeeded Hugh his father, about the year 1295. He was heritable sheriff of the County of Air, and is faid not only to have had the eftates of Loudoun, Corfbie, &c. in that **County, but alfo the eftate of** Auchinames in the fhire of Renfrew.

He fwore fealty to Edward, Auguft **5, 1296.** Henry gives him **a** moft excellent character. He was wife, of an amiable difpofition, took an affectionate concern in **the affairs of his** nephew, and was **an** affectionate brother **to lady** Wallace.

According to Henry, he was treacheroufly murder**ed at** Air, June 18, 1298.

His fons were, 1, Sir Reginald his fucceffor, who loft his life **in the** fervice of his country, in 1303; and whofe daughter, an heirefs, was married **to** Sir Duncan Campbell, anceftor of **the Campbells, Earls of** Loudoun.

2. William.

3. John, anceftor of the family of Crawfurd **of Crawfurd-land.**

4. Adam

CRAWFURD.

William Crawfurd, fecond fon of Sir Reginald, and coufin of Wallace, was compelled along with his father to fwear fealty to Edward, Auguft 5, 1296. He **was proprietor of the lands of Manwel in the** fhire of **Linlithgow.**

He was a faithful friend of Wallace, **and accompa**nied him in many of his expeditions.

Wallace

Wallace made him Governor of the town and caftle of Edinburgh. When a party was forming to drive the bifhop of Durham and others out of Scotland, William Crawfurd joined the party with three hundred men from Edinburgh, all in bright armour.

He accompanied Wallace in his firft voyage to France, who committed to him in part the guidance of the fhip, becaufe when refiding at Air he had been in ufe to mak e excurfions to fea.

He accompanied him alfo in his fecond voyage to France, and burnt the fails of the fhip of John of Lyn an Englifh pirate. He was alfo with Wallace in the battle of Black Ironfide in Fife.

He is fuppofed to have been anceftor of the Crawfurds of Haining in the fhire of Stirling, and of the Crawfurds in the fhire of Linlithgow.

CRAWFURD.

―――― Crawfurd, Laird of Kilfpindy in the Braes of the Carfe of Gowrie, Perth-fhire, and of other lands in that neighbourhood.

According to Henry, he was uncle of Hugh Crawfurd of Loudoun, and therefore in the time of Wallace muft have been a very aged man.

When Wallace and his mother were fent to him, in 1292, he protected them in his caftle at Kilfpindy, and in his houfe at Dundee; he put Wallace to the fchool at Dundee, which feems at that time to have been a fchool of confiderable reputation.

Wallace

Wallace concealed himself for some time in the Castle of Kilspindy, **after he had** killed young Selby. But the aged baron grew uneasy, and a Justice Air being to be held **at Dundee,** he was obliged to let **Wallace** and his mother **go** elsewhere, as he was no longer able to protect **them.**

In **1463,** Andrew Spens was Laird of Kilspindy. It **afterwards** belonged to a branch of **the** family of the **Earls of Angus.** Afterwards to the Lindsays. Afterwards to the Austins, of whom the last proprietor was Joseph Austin of Kilspindy, who in the war, 1757, was Captain of Marines **on** board the Monmouth, and distinguished **himself by his bravery,** February 28, 1758, when the Foudrayant was taken, the capture of which ship was reckoned **one of the** most gallant actions performed **at sea during that war.** His brother was Doctor **Adam Austin, physician in** Edinburgh.

Kilspindy, famous from its having been so long the residence of Wallace, now belongs, **by** purchase, **to** Robertson of Tullybelton.

CRAWFURD.

—— Crawfurd of Elcho in the shire of Perth, was **a near cousin of** Wallace, perhaps a son or grandson **of the old Laird** of Kilspindy.

When Wallace returned the second time from France, **he** landed with **his** companions **at the** mouth of the **river Erne, and went** with them to the Castle **of** Elcho. **Crawfurd and his** lady concealed them for

some

fome time, and were brought into much trouble on that account.

Crawfurd fought along with Wallace in the encounter with the Englifh, which happened immediately after in Elcho Park, where he was wounded in the knee, and carried off the field in Wallace's arms.

In the reign of Robert Bruce, Elcho was the property of Alexander Lord Abernethy. David Lindfay of Glenefk, anceftor of the Earls of Crawfurd, and his mother Catherine Abernethy, a co-heirefs of the above Alexander, founded a nunnery about a mile north from the caftle, on a fpot of ground which belonged to the monaftery of Dunfermling. Of this, which was called the nunnery of Elcho, there are ftill fome remains ftanding.

Elcho now belongs to the Earl of Wemyfs, and gives the title of Lord to his eldeft fon.

CURRIE.

Walter de Corry, or Currie, Knight, anceftor of the Curries of that ilk in Annandale, fwore fealty to Edward, July 13, 1296.

Adam Currie, probably his fon, came with a party to affift Wallace, about the time of the fiege of the Caftle of Sanquhar.

DICKSON.

Thomas Dickfon, a young man " bold and hardy," was a vaffal of Sir William Douglas of Douglafdale.

It

It was chiefly by his means that Sir William Douglas took the Caftle of Sanquhar. Afterwards when Sir William himfelf was befieged in that caftle, he was fent to procure the affiftance of Wallace.

The lands of Hafelfide in Douglafdale, in the fhire of Lanark, were beftowed upon him by Sir William Douglas, in reward of his many good fervices.

The Dickfons are faid to be all defcended of Richard de Keth, a fon of the family of the Earls of Marifchall.

DOUGLAS.

Sir William de Douglas, or of Douglafdale, Lord Douglas, anceftor of the noble family of Douglas, was compelled to fwear fealty to Edward, at Edinburgh, May 10, 1296.

He was an active patriot, and on many occafions the friend of Wallace. His Hiftory is well known.

DUNDAS.

Sir Elys, or Helias Dundas, was probably a brother of Saer de Dundas, anceftor of the Dundaffes of that ilk. His fifter was married to Sir John Scott, who had a large inheritance in Strathern.

He came along with Sir John Scott, and a confiderable party, to Wallace's affiftance in Elcho Park.

In the third fiege of Perth, Elys of Dundas, rafhly entered into the town. But the Earl of Fife, who was then in the town, and on the fide of the Englifh, would not allow him to be put to death. When the town

town was taken, the Earl's life was spared by the Scotish party, becaufe of the kindnefs which he had fhewed to Sir Elys Dundas.

FAWDOUN.

Fawdoun, a man of a fingular character in Henry's Poem. " He was a man of a melancholy complexion, heavy of ftature, ftern in his countenance, forrowful, fad, always dreadful without pleafance."

He, with fome others, made oath of fidelity to Wallace, in the prefence of Malcolm Earl of Lennox, September, 1296. He went with Wallace immediately after, on his firft northern expedition.

In the battle which began in Elcho Park, and which continued along the north fide of the river Erne, in November, 1296, Fawdoun ftood ftill near to the Caftle of Dupplin, faying, he was fpent with fighting, and would not move a ftep farther. Wallace, partly fufpecting his fidelity, and partly provoked by his obftinacy, ftruck off his head.

When Wallace came that night to the old Caftle of Gafk, he was much troubled in his mind, and, according to Henry, faw the ghoft of Fawdoun.

The old Caftle of Gafk was fituated about half a a mile from the prefent houfe of Gafk, nearer to the river. It is now ruinous, and is called by the people in the neighbourhood Wallace's Caftle, from the tradition of the Adventures which befel him there.

FRAZER.

Sir Simon Frazer of Oliver Caſtle in the ſhire of Peebles, was a brave patriot, and acted honourably in defence of his country. Henry only mentions his being ſent priſoner to London, while Wallace was a-live. Afterwards he joined Robert Bruce, and, being again taken priſoner, ſuffered death at London in 1306.

He left no male iſſue, and was ſucceeded by his brother Alexander, anceſtor of the Frazers of Lovat.

GORDON.

Sir Adam de Gordon, anceſtor of the Dukes of Gordon, ſwore fealty to Edward, July 28, 1296. He afterwards joined Wallace, who, in 1298, appointed him Governor of the Caſtle of Wigton in Galloway.

Wallace was Governor of Scotland, in name or behalf of the King, John Baliol. While John Baliol lived, Gordon eſpouſed his party in oppoſition to that of Bruce. But after that King's death, in 1314, he attached himſelf to Robert Bruce, and was at laſt killed in the ſervice of his country in the battle at Halidon Hill, July, 19, 1333.

GRAHAM.

" Sir John the Graham," ſays Henry, " Lord of Dundaff" in the ſhire of Stirling. He rather ſhould have ſaid " Sir David Graham," who was anceſtor of the Dukes of Montroſe.

He

He made no other bond with the Englifh, than that he fhould be allowed to live in peace, and for this, much againſt his will, he paid a tribute.

This aged baron entertained Wallace in his houfe at Dundaff, in 1296, and made his fon John fwear upon a fhield that he would be always a faithful friend of Wallace.

GRAHAM.

Sir John the Graham, fon of the above John or David. He joined Wallace in 1296, and was his faithful friend and companion in his after exploits. His heroic qualities are much celebrated.

According to Henry, he was killed in the battle at Falkirk, July 22, 1298. Wallace, " taking his dead body into his arms, and beholding his pale face, kiſſed him, and faid, my beſt brother that ever I had in the world. My fincere friend in my greateſt need. In thee was wit, freedom, and hardinefs, truth, manhood, and noblenefs."

He was buried in a Chapel at Falkirk, where, what is faid to be his epitaph, is yet to be ſeen. Viz,

" Mente Manuque potens, et Villæ filus Achates, Conditur hic Gramus, Bello interfectus ab Anglis."

" Graham is buried here, ſlain in battle by the Engliſh. He was ſtrong in mind and body, and was the faithful friend of Wallace."

Henry fays, he was married to the eldeſt daughter of Thomas Halliday, nephew of Wallace.

Gray,

GRAY.

—— Gray, probably Sir Hugh de Gray, baron of Browfield or Broxmouth in the County of Roxburgh, anceftor of the Lords of Gray in Perth fhire.

He joined Wallace in the Caftle of the Earl of Lennox in Dunbarton-fhire, September, 1296, and accompanied him immediately after, on his fiift northern expedition.

GRAY.

Mr Thomas Gray, parfon of Liberton in the fhire of Lanark, or of Liberton in Mid-Lothian, joined Wallace in 1296, and acted as his chaplain.

He is faid to have written, along with Mr John Blair, a Latin Hiftory of Wallace.

GUTHRY.

—— Guthry, anceftor of the Guthries of that ilk, was employed by the loyal party to go to France, to requeft Wallace to return to Scotland. He fought along with Wallace in the battle at Black Ironfide.

HALLIDAY.

Thomas Halliday, a celebrated patriot, was a baron of confiderable property in the fouth weft part of Scotland.

He led three hundred Annandale men in bright armour againft Edward at Biggar, in 1297. He came again with a party of men to Wallace, to affift him in

refcuing

refcuing Sir William Douglas, who was befieged in the Caſtle of Sanquhar in the fhire of Dumfries.

According to Henry, he was " fib fifter's fon to Wallace."

If he was literally nephew of Wallace, Wallace's father muſt have been twice married; for Thomas Halliday, at the time when he was affiſting Wallace, was of fuch age as to have four daughters married, viz, one to Sir John Graham younger of Dundaff, one to Sir John Johnſton in Efkdale, one to a gentleman of the furname of Wallace, and the fourth to Rutherfurd of that ilk.

HAY.

Hugh de la Hay, according to Henry, was heir of Louthowort. He fwore fealty to Edward in 1296. He made a truce with the Englifh, which laſted fome time: But about the time of the fiege of the Caſtle of Sanquhar, he joined Wallace with fifty men.

He was engaged with Wallace in many brave actions. Was fent prifoner to England while Wallace was alive. Was again taken prifoner in the battle at Methven in 1306.

His father was anceſtor of the Marquiffes of Tweedale.

JARDEN.

—— Jarden, anceſtor of the ancient family of Jarden of Applegirth in Annandale. In 1298, he joined

Wallace with a party of men which he had brought from Annandale.

JOHNSTON.

Sir John de Johnſton, anceſtor of the Marquiſſes of Annandale. Henry ſays, he was a baron of good degree in Eſkdale. Wallace appointed him Governor of the Caſtle of Lochmaben. His wife was the ſecond daughter of Thomas Halliday, nephew of Wallace.

JOP.

Jop, who is ſo often mentioned by Henry, was born at Richardtoun, in the diſtrict of Kyle in Air-ſhire. He was ſome time a purſuivant in the ſervice of King Edward, and was long in England.

Among the Engliſh, he got the name of Vot Grim-ſbe, becauſe he was of great ſtature, and of a grim countenance.

He attached himſelf early to Wallace, who employed him as his herald, and who found him of great uſe when invading England, becauſe of his exact knowledge of that country.

IRELAND.

Stephen of Ireland, or de Ireland, was born in Argyle-ſhire. His anceſtors probably had been from Ireland. He is much celebrated in Henry's Poem for his heroic deeds, and attachment to Wallace.

Ireland was a ſurname pretty common in Perth-ſhire, and there are ſtill ſome perſons who bear it.

In

In 1518, " a venerable man, Mr John Ireland, Vicar of Perth, was Dean of the Confraternity Order at Perth, an Order affumed in honour of the facred Trinity, and for the redemption of captives."

KER.

William Ker, commonly called Kerlie, or Ker Little, was anceftor of the Kers of Kerfland. He, as well as many others, was compelled to fwear the unlawful oath of fealty to Edward, Auguft 5, 1296.

He joined Wallace at the Caftle of the Earl of Lennox, September, 1296, and went with him immediately on his firft northern expedition. He and Stephen of Ireland were the only two of Wallace's men who furvived the battle along the north fide of the river Erne, November, 1296.

He was the conftant friend and companion of Wallace on all occafions, and is fometimes called his fteward. In 1305, when Wallace was taken prifoner at Robraftoun, a folitary village near Glafgow, William Ker only was with him. They were found both afleep, and Ker was killed in the fkuffle.

Henry fays, that William Ker had large inheritance in the diftrict of Carrick in Air-fhire. That his anceftor was brought from Ireland by King David I, and defeated, with the affiftance of feven hundred Scots, nine thoufand Norwegians who had landed at Dummoir. Some of the Norwegians were drowned in Doun, and others flain upon the land. King David gave him the lands of Dummoir in reward of his bravery.

It

It may be remarked, that Dun Hill, or as it is commonly called Norman or **Northman Law,** a high hill on the eftate of Dunmure, **in the** north-eaft part of **Fife,** and parifh **of** Abdie, has on the top of it the re-mains of Danifh intrenchments. The hill on the north fide, declines all the way to the river or frith of Tay, which has Dundee at the mouth of it. The conftant tradition is, that the **Danes** or Norwegians carried the fpoil of the country to the top of this hill, where the natives could have **no** accefs to them ; and after having collected it there, carried it down on the other fide to their fhips in the river.

KIRKPATRICK.

Roger de Kirkpatrick. Baron or Lord **of Tortho-rald** in the diftrict of Nith fdale and fhire of **Dumfries,** fwore fealty to Edward, in 1296. He afterwards join-ed Wallace, whofe coufin he was by his mother, **one** of the Crawfurds.

He had many difputes with the Englifh, efpecially during fix months that he abode in Eikdale wood with **twenty men.**

In King **Robert** Bruce's time, the barony **of Tor-thorald** went by **an** heirefs to Sir William **Carlyle,** an-ceftor of the Scotifh Lords of Carlyle, **the** reprefenta-tive **of** whom is Carlyle **of** Lochartur.

LAUDER.

Robert Lauder, anceftor **of** the Lauders of Bafs in Eaft-Lothian, was with Wallace in many of his ex-ploits.

ploits. On one occasion he met Wallace at Muffel-burgh, where, Henry says, " Robert Lawder keeped his place well, and neither Knight, Squire, nor Lord, could perfuade him to be at peace with Edward." He afterwards keeped the Caftle in the Ifle of Bafs.

Wallace conferred upon him the lands of Stanton, which had belonged to Sir Aymer Vallance.

It feems to be his tomb-ftone, which is to be feen in the burying-place of the Lairds of Bafs, in the old church of North Berwick.

" Hic jacet bonus Robertus Lauder, Magnus Dominus de Congleton et le Bafs, qui obiit menfe Maii, 1311." " Here lies the good Robert Lauder, the great Laird of Congleton and Bafs, who died in the month of May, 1311." Some however read it, 1411.

The family of Lauder of Bafs, continued till the reign of Charles I. The reprefentative, fays Nifbet, is Lauder of Beilmouth.

LENNOX.

Malcolm Earl of Lennox, one of the firft line of the Earls of Lennox. He maintained his territory of Len-nox in Dunbarton-fhire a long time againft the Eng-lifh, was the hofpitable friend of Wallace, and gave him much countenance and affiftance in his enterprifes.

He afterwards joined Robert Bruce, and in his old age was killed in the battle at Halidon Hill, July 19, 1333.

Haldane of Gleneagles, in the fhire of Perth, quar-ters the arms of the old Earls of Lennox, as defcended of one of the co-heireffes of Duncan the feventh Earl.

LINDSAY.

Sir William Lindfay of Craigie, fecond fon of Alexander de Lindfay Lord of Crawfurd, joined Wallace, and affifted him in his expeditions.

In the reign of David II, the heirefs of Sir John Lindfay of Craigie, married John Wallace of Richardtoun, the defcendant of the elder brother of Sir Malcolm Wallace of Ellerflie. In confequence of which marriage, the defcendants of Wallace of Richardtoun have ever fince taken the defignation of Wallace of Craigie.

Wallace of Craigie, in Henry's time, was one of thofe with whom he advifed, when writing his Poem.

LITTLE.

Edward Little. a near relation, and faithful friend of Wallace, was engaged in many brave exploits. His mother was either a fifter of Wallace, or of James Cleland of that ilk.

There were perfons in Scotland of the furname of Little, fo early as the reign of Malcolm IV. Edward Little might be anceftor of the families of Liberton and Meikledale.

LUNDIE.

Richard de Lundie, Lundin, or London, was a powerful Baron in the fhire of Fife. He brought five hundred men to Wallace's aid, in the encounter with
Macfadzan

Macfadzan near Craigmore, in Perth-fhire. On another occafion, he and Sir John the Graham, bravely fought a party of Englifh near to Bothwell, in the fhire of Lanark.

Henry however has not taken notice, that **Lundie,** having become diffatisfied with fome of the **Scotifh** leaders, was on the fide of the Englifh in the battle at Stirling Bridge, September **11, 1297.**

In a charter by King William the Lion to the town of Perth, October 10, 1210; one of the witneffes is Robert de London the King's fon, " Roberto de Londoniis Filio Meo." This natural fon of the King had married the heirefs of **Lundin in Fife,** and from her lands took his furname.

Richard was their lineal defcendant. In 1679, the family of Lundie, becaufe of their defcent, obtained liberty to bear the Royal arms of Scotland.

Afterwards, the heirefs married John Drummond Earl of Melfort, of whom, and confequently of the Earls of Perth, the honourable James Drummond of Perth is the heir and reprefentative.

LYLE.

Sir Walter Lyle, anceftor of the Lords of Lyle, was a fteady and active friend of Wallace. Henry fays, Wallace conferred on him the lands of Bridge-End-Crook. In the reign of Mary, the heirefs of the feventh Lord Lyle, married Sir Neil Montgomery of Lainfhaw, whofe defcendants were afterwards the reprefentatives of the Lords of Lyle.

Sir

MAXWELL.

Sir Herbert de Maxwell, Lord of Carlaverock in the
ſhire of Dumfries, and anceſtor of the Earls of Nithſ-
dale, ſwore fealty to Edward, in 1296.

He kept his Caſtle of Carlaverock againſt the Engliſh. When Wallace was to reſcue Sir William Douglas, who was beſieged in the Caſtle of Sanquhar, Maxwell ſent from his caſtle a party of brave men to aſſiſt
him.

MORAY.

Sir Andrew Moray, Lord of Bothwell, a brave patriot, and an early aſſociate of Wallace, was the only
perſon of note, on the ſide of the Scots, that was killed in the memorable battle at Stirling Bridge, September 11, 1297.

His repreſentative in the male line, is Moray of A-
bercairney, in the ſhire of Perth.

NEWBIGGING.

Sir Walter of Newbigging, a baron in the ſouth of
Scotland, was one of the leaders of Wallace's army
againſt Edward, at Biggar. He acted bravely, and in
the battle, had his ſon David along with him.

RAMSAY.

Sir John Ramſay of Auchter-houſe, in the ſhire of
Forfar, and heritable ſheriff there, ſwore fealty to Edward in 1296.

He

He suffered much from the English. He came to Wallace with sixty men, and was engaged with him in many enterprises. Wallace made him Governor of Perth.

Henry enlarges in giving a character of his son. " His son Alexander," says he, " was called the Flower of Courtlinefs. He made a great figure in the time of Bruce. In war, he was one of the braveft of men, and in time of peace, gave himfelf to Courtlinefs; fo that any gentleman who had not been in the company of Alexander Ramfay, was not reckoned polite. He took the Caftle of Roxburgh from the English, and held it till he was treacheroufly put to death. He was a lover of freedom and truth, and there never had been a more worthy gentleman in Scotland than he was."

Fordun, fpeaking of this Alexander Ramfay, fays, " he was called the Flower of Chevalry," and that the young nobles thought they could have no character for bravery and military fkill, unlefs they had been with him in his excurfions. He fuffered a cruel death in 1342.

Henry fays, he was the fon of Sir John Ramfay of Auchter-houfe, and Fordun fays nothing in contradiction.

In the reign of Robert II, the heirefs of this family, married Patrick Ogilvy, anceftor of the Earls of Airlie, who thereby was denominated of Auchter-houfe.

In the reign of James III, the heirefs of Ogilvy of Auchter-houfe, married James Stewart Earl of Buchan, who

who upon that account, acquired the additional title of Lord Auchter-houfe.

In the reign of James VI, the heirefs of Buchan and Auchter-houfe, married James Erfkine, fecond fon of the Earl of Mar, and anceftor of the Erfkines, Earls of Buchan.

RANDULPH.

Sir Thomas Randulph, Earl of Murray, Lord of the Valley of Annan, and of the Ifle of Man, was fon of Thomas Ranulph of Strathdon, by Ifabel Bruce, fifter of King Robert Bruce.

He obtained his titles from the King his uncle, in reward of his fingular good fervices.

Henry only fpeaks of him as a patriot, who, along with fome others, was fent prifoner to London. The time when he made the greateft figure, was during the wars of Robert Bruce.

After that King's death, in 1329, he was made Regent of the Kingdom, and died in 1332.

In the reign of David II, the reprefentation of the Randulphs, Earls of Murray, devolved, by the marriage of the heirefs, on the Dunbars, Earls of March.

RUTHERFURD.

Sir Nichol de Rutherfurd, anceftor of the Rutherfurds of that ilk in the fhire of Roxburgh, fwore fealty to Edward, in 1296.

According to Henry, his wife was a daughter of Thomas Halliday, and therefore a near relation of Wallace.

Wallace. When he firſt joined Wallace, he came a-
long with his father-in-law, and fought againſt Edward in the battle at Biggar.

Afterwards, when Sir William Douglas was to be
relieved, who was beſieged in the Caſtle of Sanquhar,
and who had aſked the aſſiſtance of Wallace and his
party, Henry ſays, " Good Rutherfurd, who had always been true againſt the Engliſh, and who had done
them much harm while he was abiding in Ettrick
wood, came to Wallace, with ſixty noble, or brave
men in warlike array."

His ſon Sir Robert de Rutherfurd, Dominus de eo-
dem, or Lord of that ilk, ſignalized himſelf in the ſervice of his country, in the time of King Robert Bruce.

In the reign of James IV, a daughter of this family
having married James Stewart, anceſtor of the Earls
of Traquair, was the occaſion of a part of the lands
going to the family of Traquair. But her uncle Thomas, as heir male, retained the lands of Edgerſtone
and others, and he and his heirs continued the deſig-
nation of Rutherfurds of that ilk.

Andrew Rutherfurd, Earl of Teviot and the Lords
of Rutherfurd, were branches of this family.

The laſt Lord Rutherfurd, who died in 1724, and
who is ſaid to have had by the patent, a right to diſ-
poſe of his title. if he had pleaſed even in his laſt mo-
ments, made a diſpoſition, ſome years before his death,
of his eſtates and title to the family of Edgerſtone,
from which he originally ſprung. They have ſince

poffeffed the eftates, but none of them have yet taken up the title, though others have been claiming it.

RUTHVEN.

Sir William Ruthven, Baron of Ruthven, now called Hunting-tower, two miles weft from Perth, anceftor of the Lords of Ruthven, and Earls of Gowrie, was compelled along with others, to fwear allegiance to Edward, in 1296.

Henry fays, he was a true Scots patriot. The firft time Perth was befieged by Wallace, Ruthven brought to his affiftance thirty brave men, who had often tried their weapons againft the enemy.

He was with Sir Chriftopher Seton in taking Jedburgh from the Englifh. and, with the confent of Wallace, was left Governor there. When a powerful army was gathering, to expel the Englifh from Scotland, Ruthven brought out of Jedburgh a numerous body of Teviotdale men.

After Wallace's firft return from France, Ruthven, who had been lurking in Birnam wood, came to affift in the fecond fiege of Perth. Wallace, he, and fome others difguifed themfelves as peafants, and got admiffion into the town. Wallace immediately, in reward of his good fervices, made him fheriff of Perth, an office which continued to be hereditary in his family.

He married Marjory, daughter of the patriotic Sir John Ramfay of Auchter-houfe, and died in 1320.

Sir

SCOTT.

Sir John Scott, a Baron in Strathern, and whom Wallace calls a worthy Knight, joined Wallace after his second return from France. He endured, along with Wallace, many hardships in the west Highlands, and affisted in the third siege of Perth.

He was probably a descendant of the family of Scott of Balweary in Fife. And according to Henry, he was married to a fister of Sir Elys Dundas.

The family of Scott of Balweary continued till the reign of Charles I. That family is now reprefented by the Scotts of Ancrum, in Roxburgh-fhire.

SCRYMGEOUR.

Sir Alexander Scrymgeour, anceftor of the Vifcounts of Dudhope, and of the Earl of Dundee, bore the royal ftandard in Wallace's battles.

In a written deed, dated at Torphichen, in Weft-Lothian, March 28, 1298, he was appointed by Wallace Conftable of Dundee, which office continued to be hereditary in the family.

After Wallace's death, he joined the intereft of Robert Bruce. The reprefentative of the family, is Scrymgeour of Birk-hill.

SETON.

Sir Chriftopher Seton, anceftor of the Earls of Winton, was a fteady patriot, and a friend of. Wallace. Many of his brave actions are recounted by Henry.

He married **Lady Chriſtian Bruce, ſiſter** of King **Robert** Bruce, and was **cruelly put to death at Dumfries,** by order of Edward, **in 13c6.**

The repreſentation of the family of Winton **is in** Sir George Seton **of** Garleton.

SINCLAIR.

William Sinclair, the patriotic biſhop of **Dunkeld,** and **the friend** of Wallace, was **a younger ſon of Sir William** Sinclair **of** Roſlin; anceſtor **of the Earls of** Orkney.

According to **Henry,** who recounts many of his **acts of** patriotiſm, **he had been** elected to the ſee of Dunkeld in **Wallace's time, but was kept from the poſſeſ-ſion** by **the Engliſh.**

SOMMERVILLE.

Sir Thomas de Sommerville of Linton and Carnwath, **anceſtor** of the Lords of Sommerville, ſwore fealty to Edward, May 15, **1296.** He joined Wallace, July, **1297.** Henry ſays, he was **of** great renown, and aſſiſted **Wallace in** defeating King Edward at Biggar.

STEWART.

Sir James the Stewart of Scotland. According **to Henry, when Wallace went to France, he left Lord James Stewart Governor of Scotland in his abſence.**

He was father of Walter, who married the Princeſs Marjory, daughter of King Robert Bruce, and was therefore one of the anceſtors of the royal family of Stewart.

Sir

TINTO.

Sir John of Tinto in the weft of Scotland, was a brave patriot, and a friend of Wallace. Henry relates fome of his exploits.

WALLACE.

Sir Richard Wallace of Richardtoun, in the fhire of Air, was of an ancient family, fuppofed to be of Welch extraction. He frequently protected his nephew Wallace at his houfe, and was blind fome years before his death, owing to wounds he had received in battle.

He died in 1298, and was fucceeded by his eldeft fon Adam.

WALLACE.

Adam Wallace of Richardtoun, fon of Sir Richard, fwore fealty to Edward, Auguft 5, 1296. He was then only about eighteen years of age.

He was engaged with his coufin Wallace, in many brave actions. Henry fays of him that he was " of large ftature, wife, worthy, and brave; that he was long in the wars of King Robert Bruce, who made him a Knight for his good fervices."

Near the end of the reign of David II, John Wallace of Richardtoun, fon or grandfon of this Adam, married the heirefs of John Lindfay of Craigie, and was thereupon afterwards defigned of Craigie, as his defcendants fince have been.

The

The family of Wallace of Craigie, or Richardtoun, received the honour of Knight Baronet, in 1669.

WALLACE.

Richard and Simon, were younger fons of Sir Richard Wallace of Richardtoun. Richard, in the time of Wallace, came to be of fuch an age, as to be capable of affifting him in fome of his exploits.

WALLACE.

Sir Malcolm Wallace of Ellerflie, in the fhire of Renfrew, was a younger brother of Sir Richard Wallace of Richardtoun. He was married to Margaret Crawfurd, daughter of Hugh Crawfurd of Loudoun, and by her was father of Sir William Wallace, who on account of his bravery and loyalty, was chofen Governor of Scotland, and General of its armies, under the king, John Baliol.

Sir Malcolm probably had been married to another lady, before his marriage with Margaret Crawfurd. By his former lady, he had Malcolm his apparent heir. Alfo two daughters, one of whom was married to the father of Thomas Halliday, and the other to the father of Edward Little.

Sir Malcolm, and his fon Malcolm, were killed in a battle with the Englifh on Loudoun Hill, in 1295. The right of fucceffion to the eftate of Ellerflie thereby belonged to his other fon William. Since that time, Ellerflie has fometimes belonged to the family of Wallace

lace of Craigie or Richardton, and fometimes to branches of that family.

WALLACE.

Sir William Wallace of **Ellerflie,** fon of Sir Malcolm,
as before mentioned, **was,** according **to Henry, born**
in or about the **year** 1267. He had all the qualificati-
ons **neceffary at** that time to conftitute the character
of a hero. He had a paffion for liberty, a love to **his**
country, and had received great provocati**ons from** the
Englifh, who had killed his father, and elder brother,
and others his near relations.

From being a private **difturber of the** Englifh, **he** became their public, **and legally authorifed** opponent.
The title which he **bore, in 1298, was,** " Willelmus
Walays **Miles.** Cuftos Regni **Scotiæ, et Ductor Ex-**
ercituum ejufdem, nomine præclari Principis Domini
Johannis, Dei Gratia, Regis Scotiæ illuftris, **de Con-**
fenfu Communitatis ejufdem."

" William Wallas **Knight,** governor of the King-
dom of Scotland, **and Leader of** its armies, in name of
of an excellent **Prince, Lord John, by** the Grace of
God the illuftrious King of Scotland, and by the con-
fent of the Community of the fame."

Henry fays, **that in April, 1297, the Scotifh patri-**
ots, who were in arms **at the time, made choice of**
Wallace for their chief. Afterwards they held a council at Braidwood **three days,** and appointed a folemn
national convention to affemble at Selkirk, or, as he

calls

calls it, the Foreſt Kirk, in July, 1297. In that convention, Wallace was elected " Warden of Scotland."

It is not improbable what Henry ſays, that after his
ſucceſſes, the great Barons envied his ſituation, and
that Robert Bruce entertained ſuſpicions of his aiming
at the Crown.

Henry, in one part of his Poem, ſays, that Wallace
continued in keen debate in behalf of Scotland, exactly ſix years and ſeven months. Yet he repreſents him
as almoſt conſtantly employed in valorous acts againſt
the Engliſh, either at home, in England, or in France,
from ſome time in 129c, till July, 13c5, when he was
taken priſoner, and ſent to London.

Johannes Major, and after him the accurate writer
of " the Annals of Scotland," ſeem to have taken ſome
pains in giving a faithful account of him.

Major, however doubts his voyages to France. But
Fordun, according to the Perth and Cupar Manuſ-
cripts of the Scotichronicon, affirms that he went to
France, where he acquired honour in fighting againſt
the Engliſh there, and that in his way to France he
encountered pirates, for which a reference is made to
the vulgar Scots and French ſongs.

Henry repreſents him as having been the deliverer
of Scotland three ſeveral times. It appears beyond all
controverſy, that once at leaſt, viz, after the battle at
Stirling Bridge, September 11, 1297. he was the deliverer of his country.

Wallace was tried, as a traitor againſt the King of
England, in Weſtminſter Hall, Auguſt 23, 13c5. He
denied

denied that he was such a traitor, for he never had owed any obedience to Edward. But he acknowledged all that he was charged with as having done againft the Englifh. He was crowned with laurel, in a way of mockery, during his trial, as other Scotifh patriots were whom Edward put to death.

Henry fays, he was thirty days a prifoner in London before his death. He maintained his unconquerable fpirit to the laft, and the Englifhmen, in a jefting manner, faid, that he felt no pain.

His head was fixed upon London Bridge, and his legs and arms were fent to Scotland, his right leg to be put up at Perth, and his left at Aberdeen.

John Speed, an old Englifh writer, fays, " though we" (viz, we who are Englifh), " do not call Wallace a martyr, yet muft we think his country honoured in him, wifhing many the like in our own." Speed's Hift. p. 66c.

WALLACE.

—— Wallace, Parfon of Dunipace in the fhire of Stirling, was a younger brother of Sir Richard Wallace of Richardtoun.

Henry fays, " he had great riches." He entertained in his houfe at Dunipace, his nephew Wallace and his mother, when they were flying from Perth-fhire, in 129c. He again entertained him, and fupplied him liberally, after his firft northern expedition, November, 1295. Afterwards he was put into a wet dungeon

geon in the Caftle of Airth in Stirling-fhire, out of which he was delivered by his nephew.

Henry relates fome conferences in which the prieft of Dunipace, reckoning the Scotifh caufe irrecoverable, advifed Wallace to fubmit to Edward. But the early inftructions he had given to Wallace, rendered it impoflible for him to follow fuch an advice.

Fordun relates, L. 12. C. 3. that when Edward had made very liberal offers to Wallace, to induce him to fubmit, as many others of his countrymen had done, and when fome of Wallace's own friends were endeavouring to perfuade him to comply, Wallace, with much emotion, anfwered, " O defolated Scotland, too credulous of fair fpeeches, and not aware of the calamities which are coming upon you! If you were to judge as I do, you would not eafily put your neck under a foreign yoke.

" When I was a boy, the prieft, my uncle, carefully inculcated upon me this proverb, which I then learned. and have ever fince kept in my mind :

" Dico tibi verum, Libertas optima Rerum :
Nunquam fervili fub Nexu vivito Fili."

" I tell you a truth, Liberty is the beft of things. My fon, never live under any flavifh bond."

" Therefore I fhortly declare, that if all others, the natives of Scotland, fhould obey the King of England, or were to part with the Liberty which belongs to them, I and my affociates, who may be willing to adhere to me in this point, will ftand for the Liberty of

the

the Kingdom ; and, by God's affiftance, will only obey the King" (viz, John Baliol), " or his Lieutenant."

WATSON.

John Watfon, a gentleman in the fouth-weft part of Scotland, being well acquainted with the town and Caftle of Lochmaben in the fhire of Dumfries, was employed by Thomas Halliday in taking that Caftle by furprife.

(N. B. It is obvious that many particulars, mentioned in the above Lift, depend on the authority of Henry.)

ASCRIBED to WALLACE.

HENRY, B. 9. v. 1912, gives a defcription of Wallace's perfon. He was to appearance more than fix foot high, and his body was otherwife large, and well proportioned.

All the old Scots writers takes notice of his great bodily ftrength. Henry always keeps it in view, in whatever he relates concerning him.

There can be no doubt that he poffeffed this perfonal property in fome eminent degree. It was neceffary to the advancement of his character, and fortune, at a time, when battles were fought chiefly in the manner of fingle combats. Without a confiderable fhare of it, no military man, however brave, could expect to be much feared, or honoured.

There is an anecdote, in confirmation of the uncommon degree of ftrength afcribed to Wallace, related by Hector Boeis. Though Boeis be in general an author not much to be credited, yet it would be hard not to believe him in an inftance which happened near his own time, and in which, if he had fpoken falfely, he could immediately have been detected.

The anecdote in another refpect is curious, as it affords an example of longevity, fimilar to that of the Irifh Countefs of Defmond.

The date is the end of the year 1430. At that time King James I, returned to Perth from St Andrews, where he had been vifiting the Univerfity; and having

perhaps

perhaps heard Henry, as a visiter in his Court, recite some of Wallace's exploits, found his curiosity excited to visit a noble lady of great age, who was able to inform him of many ancient matters.

She lived in the Castle of Kinnoul, on the opposite side of the river from Perth; and was probably the widow of one of the Lords of Erskine, a branch of whose family, continued to be denominated from the Barony of Kinnoul, till about the year 1440.

It was Boeis' way to relate an event as circumstantially, as if he himself had been one of the persons present, and engaged in it. I shall therefore give the anecdote in his own manner, by translating his own words.

" In consequence of her extreme old age, she had lost her sight: But all her other senses were entire, and her body was yet firm and lively. She had seen William Wallace, and Robert Bruce, and frequently told particulars concerning them.

" The King, who entertained a love and veneration of great men, resolved to visit the old lady, that he might hear her describe the manners and strength of the two heroes, who were admired in his time, as they now are in ours. He therefore sent a message, acquainting her, that he was to come to her the next day.

" She received the message gratefully, and gave immediate orders to her handmaids, to prepare every thing for his reception, in the best manner; particularly, that they should display her pieces of tapestry, some of which were uncommonly rich and beautiful.

And

And she strictly enjoined, that every thing should be removed, which could give any offence to the delicate eyes of the courtiers.

" All her servants became busily employed, for their work was in some degree unusual, as she had not of a long time been accustomed to receive princely visiters.

" The next day, when told the King was approaching, she went down into the hall of her castle, dressed with as much elegance and finery as her old age, and the fashion of the time would permit ; attended by a train of matrons, many of whom were her own descendants, of which number some appeared much more altered and disfigured by age, than she herself was.

" One of her matrons having informed her that the King was entering the hall, she rose from her seat, and advanced to meet him, so easily and gracefully, that he doubted of her being wholly blind. At his desire, she embraced and kissed him.

" Her attendants assured him that she was wholly blind, and that from long custom, she had acquired these easy movements.

" He took her by the hand, and sat down, desiring her to sit on the seat next to him. And then, in a long conference, he interrogated her about ancient matters.

" He was much delighted with her conversation. Among other things, he asked her to tell him what sort of a man William Wallace was. What was his personal figure ? What his courage ? And with what degree of strength he was endowed ? He put the same questions to her concerning Robert Bruce.

" Robert,

" Robert, faid fhe, was a man beautiful, and of a fine appearance. His ftrength was fo great, that he could eafily have overcome any, mortal man of his time. But in fo far as he excelled other men, he was excelled by Wallace, both in ftature, and in bodily ftrength: For, in wreftling, Wallace could have overthrown two fuch men as Robert was.

" The King made fome enquiries concerning his own immediate parents, and his other anceftors; and having heard her relate many things, returned to Perth, well pleafed with the vifit he had made." (Boeth. Hift. L. 17.)

The Lady Erfkine, as I think fhe may be called, could not have been lefs than a hundred and thirty years of age, at the time Boeis mentions.

Mr Henry Adamfon, who wrote near the beginning of the laft century, who was brother of Mr John Adamfon Principal of the College of Edinburgh, and nephew, or grandfon, of Patrick Adamfon Archbifhop of St Andrews, in the Sixth Book of his " Mufe's Threnodie," defcribes the fituation of this Lady's Caftle. He reprefents it as fituated a little to the fouthward, " on the bank of the river Tay, with fhady woods on the high ground to the eaft, and green meadows fpread below."

He relates what were fome traditionary ftories concerning her in his time, particularly fome things honourable to the family of Hay, who became, in his time, the noble proprietors of the eftate of Kinnoul.

SUBSCRIBERS NAMES.

** *None of the Bookfellers or others, who took in Sub-fcriptions, have fent the Names to the Publifhers, for which reafon, only thofe who Subfcribed with R. Morifon and Son could be inferted in the following Lift.*

ANTIQUARIAN Society. Perth, 6 copies.
Mr James Alexander, Dunfermling.
Thomas Anderfon, Efq; Perth.
Mr John Anderfon, Glafgow
Robert Aird, Efq; Crofs-flatt, 7 copies.
Mr W. Aird, Saddler, Glafgow.

The Rt. Honourable The Earl of Buchan, 5 copies.
Mr Alexander Bell, Perth.
The Revd. Mr David Black, St Madoes.
Mr Thomas Black, Perth.
Lady Sarah Bruce Stobhall.
Mr William Blair, Perth.
Mr Thomas Beveridge, do.
Mr George Bartie, do
Mr Robert Burns, Ellifland.
Mr Henry Buift, Perth.
Mr Dugald Bannatyne, Glafgow.
Mr Peter Buchanan, do.
Mr James Bowman, do.
Robert Bailie, Efq; Carpin.

John Campbell, Efq; Taymount.
Mr Geo. Condie, Perth.
Mr John Caw, Junior, do
Sir James Colquhoun, Baronet.
Mr John Campbell, Perth.
John Cunningham, Efq; Dumfries, 5 copies.
Joseph Campbell Efq; Kinloch.
Mr James Chalmers, Perth.
Mr William Corbett, Stirling.
Mr Charles Cowan, Leith.
Mr James Cochran, Down.

Mr James Cooper, Edinburgh.
Lady Susan Carnegie.
P. Colquhoun, Esq; Glasgow.

The Honourable Mrs Drummond of Perth.
The Honourable Miss Drummond, Machany.
David Dale, Esq; Glasgow.
Mr James Davidson, Edinburgh.
Mr Dunbar, Leith.
George Dempster, Esq; Dunnichen.
Mr Neil Douglas, Cupar-Fyffe.
Mr James Donaldson, Edinburgh.
The Revd. Mr Dowe, Methven.
Mr William Dunn, Airth.

The Right Honourable Lord Elgin.
D. Erskine. Esq; Edinburgh, 2 copies.
Ja. Fr. Erskine, Esq; Dalhozine.

W. Farquharson, Esq; Dungarthill.
Captain Freer, Innernethy.
E. Fergusson, Esq; Baledmont.
Samuel Falconer, Esq; Nairn.

Mr Alexander Graham, Glasgow.
Mr John Gibson, do.
Mr John Gillies, Perth, 6 copies.
Patrick Greenhill, Esq; Balmossie.
Miss Clem. Graham, Pitarowes.
Mr Humphry Graham, Lune Craigs.
The Revd Mr George Gleig, Stirling.

George Haldane, Esq; Gleneagles.
Gilbert Hamilton, Esq; Glasgow.

Mr W. Ireland, Limekills.
The Revd. Mr J Inglis, Tippermuir.
The Revd. Mr James Leslie, Fordown, 5 copies.

Sir Thomas Moncrieff. Baronet.
James Murray, Esq; Perth.
Mr John M'Omie, do.

Mr

Mr John Menzies, **Perth.**
Mr Thomas **Mitchell, do.**
John Murray, Efq; Murray's-Hall.
George Melifs, Efq; 2 copies.
James Millar, Efq; **Glafgow.**
Mr Thomas H. Marfhall, **Perth.**
Mr David M'Vicar, Stanley.
Mr David M'Intyre, Oban.
The Revd. Mr Murray, **Perth.**
Mr James Mundell, Dumfries.
Mr James M'Laren, Perth.
Mr John M'Ewen, Glafgow.
Mr Peter Murdoch, do.
Mr John Maxwell, do.
Mr Walter Miller, Perth.
James M'Neil, Efq; Stirling.

Archibald Neilfon, Efq; Dundee.

Laurence Oliphant, Efq; Gafk.

George Paterfon, Efq; Caftle-Huntly.
The Revd. Mr Adam Peebles, Perth.
Mr James Paton, do.
Mr James Peddie Surgeon.

Mr William Ranken, Perth.
Mr James Reoch, Leith.

The Revd. Mr James Scott, Prefident of the Antiqua-
  rian Society, Perth.
Sir William Stirling. Baronet, Airdoch.
Mr Archibald Smith, Glafgow.
Mr Walter Stirling, do.
Mr William Strothers, do.
Dr Smyth, Innerpaffry.
Mr Adam Stobie, Perth.
Mr David Sherriff Kinmillies
Mr David Sherriff Drimhills.
John Stewart, Efq; Tay Bank.
Mr William Stewart, Perth.
Mr John Sandeman, Luncarty.

Robert

Robert Stewart, Efq ; Caftle Stewart, 2 copies.
Mifs Sandeman, Perth.
Dr Stewart. Dunkeld.
Mr John Sime, Perth.
Mr William Small, do.

W. Tytler, Efq ; Edinburgh.
Sir John Wedderburn, Baronet, Balindean.
Mr Alexander Watfon, Perth.
Mr James Wright, Junior, Dundee.
Mr Patrick Wright, Glafgow.
Mr Thomas Wood, Perth.
Mr David Walker, do.
Mr Andrew Wallace, Junior, Stirling.

Mr John Young, Perth.
Mr John Young, Writer to the Signet, Edinburgh.

Mr Alexander Mollison, **Edinburgh.**
Mr Murray of Simprim.
Mr Hugh Robertson.
Mr John Geddis, 5 copies.
·Mr Newbegging.
Mr Patrick Duff.
Mr Thomas Napier, Montrose
Mr Cunningham, Jeweller.
Robert Arbuthnot Esq ;
Lieut. Col. Hepburn, Keith.
Mr John Mack.
Mr John Irving.
Mr Forsyth.
William Fullarton of Carstairs **Esq ;**
Mr Londin. Bruntssiington.
Collector Ogilvy, do.
Mr William Hodge, Falkirk,
Mr George Hunter.
Kenneth Murchison of Taradale **Esq ;**
Mr William Robertson.
Mr Rose, **New Edinburgh.**
Mr Cochrane.
Mr M'Kenzie.
William Copland of Colleston Esq ; 2 copies,
Mr Handyside, **Merchant.**
Mr Irvine.
Mr Lawder, **North Berwick.**
Mr Walter Boston.
Mr Keddie.
Mr Campbell Adie, W. S.
Mr Thomson. .
Captain Cowie.
Sir G. Hume.
Mr John M'Intyre, Writer, Leith.
Mr Forsyth Bookseller in Elgin, 4 copies,
Mr Alexander Elspin, Langholm.
Mr Wallace.
Mr N Wallace, Cabinet Maker.
Mr Dundass.
Mr Dallas.
Mr Ross.

Mr Alexander M Lachan.
Mr Iſaac Forſyth. Kelſo, 5 copies.
Doctor George Monro.
Mr M'Gregor.
Mr John Bell, Air.

www.ingramcontent.com/pod-product-compliance
Lightning Source LLC
Chambersburg PA
CBHW021112020726
47500CB00003B/730